Touch and Go by D. H. Lawrence

A PLAY IN THREE ACTS

For many of us DH Lawrence was a schoolboy hero. Who can forget sniggering in class at the mention of Women In Love or Lady Chatterley's Lover? Lawrence was a talented if nomadic writer whose novels were passionately received, suppressed at times and generally at odds with Establishment values. This of course did not deter him. At his death in 1930 at the young age of 44 he was more often thought of as a pornographer but in the ensuing years he has come to be more rightly regarded as one of the most imaginative writers these shores have produced. As well as his novels he was also a masterful poet and wrote over 800 of them. Here we publish his plays. Once again Lawrence shows his hand as a brilliant writer. Delving into situations and peeling them back to reveal the inner heart.

Index Of Contents

CHARACTERS
GERALD BARLOW
MR BARLOW (his father)
OLIVER TURTON
JOB ARTHUR FREER
WILLIE HOUGHTON
ALFRED BREFFITT
WILLIAM (a butler)
CLERKS, MINERS, etc.
ANABEL WRATH
MRS BARLOW
WINIFRED BARLOW
EVA (a maid)

Schedule
ACT I
SCENE I: Market-place of a Midland mining village
SCENE II: Winifred's studio at Lilley Close

ACT II
Drawing-room at Lilley Close

ACT III
SCENE I: An old park
SCENE II: Same as Act I Scene I

ACT I

SCENE I

Sunday morning. Market-place of a large mining village in the Midlands. A man addressing a small gang of colliers from the foot of a stumpy memorial obelisk. Church bells heard. Churchgoers passing along the outer pavements.

WILLIE HOUGHTON: What's the matter with you folks, as I've told you before, and as I shall keep on telling you every now and again, though it doesn't make a bit of difference, is that you've got no idea of freedom whatsoever. I've lived in this blessed place for fifty years, and I've never seen the spark of an idea, nor of any response to an idea, come out of a single one of you, all the time. I don't know what it is with colliers, whether it's spending so much time in the bowels of the earth, but they never seem to be able to get their thoughts above their bellies. If you've got plenty to eat and drink, and a bit over to keep the missis quiet, you're satisfied. I never saw such a satisfied bloomin' lot in my life as you Barlow and Walsall's men are, really. Of course you can growse as well as anybody, and you do growse. But you don't do anything else. You're stuck in a sort of mud of contentment, and you feel yourselves sinking, but you make no efforts to get out. You bleat a bit, like sheep in a bog, but you like it, you know. You like sinking in, you don't have to stand on your own feet then.

I'll tell you what'll happen to you chaps. I'll give you a little picture of what you'll be like in the future. Barlow and Walsall's 'll make a number of compounds, such as they keep niggers in in South Africa, and there you'll be kept. And every one of you'll have a little brass collar round his neck, with a number on it. You won't have names any more. And you'll go from the compound to the pit, and from the pit back again to the compound. You won't be allowed to go outside the gates, except at weekends. They'll let you go home to your wives on Saturday nights, to stop over Sunday. But you'll have to be in again by half-past nine on Sunday night; and if you're late, you'll have your next week-end knocked off. And there you'll be, and you'll be quite happy. They'll give you plenty to eat, and a can of beer a day, and a bit of bacca, and they'll provide dominoes and skittles for you to play with. And you'll be the most contented set of men alive. But you won't be men. You won't even be animals. You'll go from number one to number three thousand, a lot of numbered slaves, a new sort of slaves

VOICE: An' wheer shall thee be, Willie?

WILLIE: Oh, I shall be outside the palings, laughing at you. I shall have to laugh, because it'll be your own faults. You'll have nobody but yourself to thank for it. You don't want to be men. You'd rather not be free, much rather. You're like those people spoken of in Shakespeare: "Oh, how eager these men are to be slaves!" I believe it's Shakespeare, or the Bible, one or the other, it mostly is

ANABEL WRATH (passing to church): It was Tiberius.

WILLIE: Eh?

ANABEL: Tiberius said it.

WILLIE: Tiberius! Oh, did he? (Laughs.) Thanks! Well, if Tiberius said it, there must be something in it. And he only just missed being in the Bible, anyway. He was a day late, or they'd have had him in. "Oh, how eager these men are to be slaves!" It's evident the Romans deserved all they got from Tiberius and you'll deserve all you get, every bit of it. But don't you bother, you'll get it. You won't be at the mercy of Tiberius, you'll be at the mercy of something a jolly sight worse. Tiberius took the skin off a few Romans, apparently. But you'll have the soul taken out of you, every one of you. And I'd rather lose my skin than my soul, any day. But perhaps you wouldn't.

VOICE: What art makin' for, Willie? Tha seems to say a lot, but tha goes round it. Tha'rt like a donkey on a gin. Tha gets ravelled.

WILLIE: Yes, that's just it. I am precisely like a donkey on a gin, a donkey that's trying to wind a lot of colliers up to the surface. There's many a donkey that's brought more colliers than you up to see daylight, by trotting round. But do you want to know what I'm making for? I can soon tell you that. You Barlow and Walsall's men, you haven't a soul to call your own. Barlow and Walsall's have only to say to one of you, Come, and he cometh; Go, and he goeth, Lie down and be kicked, and he lieth down and he is kicked and serve him jolly well right.

VOICE: Ay, an' what about it? Tha's got a behind o' thy own, hasn't ter?

WILLIE: Do you stand there and ask me what about it, and haven't the sense to alter it? Couldn't you set up a proper Government to-morrow, if you liked? Couldn't you contrive that the pits belonged to you, instead of you belonging to the pits, like so many old pit-ponies that stop down till they are blind, and take to eating coal-slack for meadow-grass, not knowing the difference? If only you'd learn to think, I'd respect you. As you are, I can't, not if I try my hardest. All you can think of is to ask for another shilling a day. That's as far as your imagination carries you. And perhaps you get sevenpence ha'penny, but pay for it with half a crown's worth of sweat. The masters aren't fools, as you are. They'll give you two-thirds of what you ask for, but they'll get five-thirds of it back again, and they'll get it out of your flesh and blood, too, in jolly hard work. Shylock wasn't in it with them. He only wanted a pound of flesh. But you cheerfully give up a pound a week, each one of you, and keep on giving it up. But you don't seem to see these things. You can't think beyond your dinners and your 'lowance. You think if you can get another shilling a day you're set up. You make me tired, I tell you.

JOB ARTHUR FREER: We think of others besides ourselves.

WILLIE: Hello, Job Arthur, are you there? I didn't recognise you without your frock-coat and silk hat, on the Sabbath. What was that you said? You think of something else, besides yourselves? Oh ay, I'm glad to hear it. Did you mean your own importance?

A motor car, GERALD BARLOW driving, OLIVER TURTON with him, has pulled up.

JOB ARTHUR (glancing at the car): No, I didn't.

WILLIE: Didn't you, though? Come, speak up, let us have it. The more the merrier. You were going to say something.

JOB ARTHUR: Nay, you were doing the talking.

WILLIE: Yes, so I was, till you interrupted, with a great idea on the tip of your tongue. Come, spit it out. No matter if Mr Barlow hears you. You know how sorry for you we feel, that you've always got to make your speeches twice, once to those above, and once to us here below. I didn't mean the angels and the devils, but never mind. Speak up, Job Arthur.

JOB ARTHUR: It's not everybody as has as much to say as you, Mr Houghton.

WILLIE: No, not in the open, that's a fact. Some folks says a great deal more, in semi-private. You were just going to explain to me, on behalf of the men, whom you so ably represent and so wisely lead, Job Arthur, we won't say by the nose, you were just going to tell me, on behalf of the men, of course, not of the masters, that you think of others, besides yourself. Do you mind explaining what others?

JOB ARTHUR: Everybody's used to your talk, Mr Houghton, and for that reason it doesn't make much impression. What I meant to say, in plain words, was that we have to think of what's best for everybody, not only for ourselves.

WILLIE: Oh, I see. What's best for everybody! I see! Well, for myself, I'm much obliged, there's nothing for us to do, gentlemen, but for all of us to bow acknowledgments to Mr Job Arthur Freer, who so kindly has all our interests at heart.

JOB ARTHUR: I don't profess to be a red-rag Socialist. I don't pretend to think that if the Government had the pits it would be any better for us. No. What I mean is, that the pits are there, and every man on this place depends on them, one way or another. They're the cow that gives the milk. And what I mean is, how every man shall have a proper share of the milk, which is food and living. I don't want to kill the cow and share up the meat. It's like killing the goose that laid the golden egg. I want to keep the cow healthy and strong. And the cow is the pits, and we're the men that depend on the pits.

WILLIE: Who's the cat that's going to lick the cream?

JOB ARTHUR: My position is this, and I state it before masters and men, that it's our business to strike such a balance between the interests of the men and the interests of the masters that the pits remain healthy, and everybody profits.

WILLIE: You're out for the millennium, I can see, with Mr Job Arthur Freer striking the balance. We all see you, Job Arthur, one foot on either side of the fence, balancing the see-saw, with masters at one end and men at the other. You'll have to give one side a lot of pudding. But go back a bit, to where we were before the motor car took your breath away. When you said, Job Arthur, that you think of others besides yourself, didn't you mean, as a matter of fact, the office men? Didn't you mean that the colliers, led, we won't mention noses, by you, were going to come out in sympathy with the office clerks, supposing they didn't get the rise in wages which they've asked for, the office clerks? Wasn't that it?

JOB ARTHUR: There's been some talk among the men of standing by the office. I don't know what they'll do. But they'll do it of their own decision, whatever it is.

WILLIE: There's not a shadow of doubt about it, Job Arthur. But it's a funny thing the decisions all have the same foxy smell about them, Job Arthur.

OLIVER TURTON (calling from the car): What was the speech about, in the first place?

WILLIE: I beg pardon?

OLIVER: What was the address about, to begin with?

WILLIE: Oh, the same old hat. Freedom. But partly it's given to annoy the Unco Guid, as they pass to their Sabbath banquet of self-complacency.

OLIVER: What about Freedom?

WILLIE: Very much as usual, I believe. But you should have been here ten minutes sooner, before we began to read the lessons. (Laughs.)

ANABEL W. (moving forward, and holding out her hand): You'd merely have been told what Freedom isn't: and you know that already. How are you, Oliver?

OLIVER: Good God, Anabel! are you part of the meeting? How long have you been back in England?

ANABEL: Some months, now. My family have moved here, you know.

OLIVER: Your family! Where have they moved from? from the moon?

ANABEL: No, only from Derby. How are you, Gerald?

GERALD twists in his seat to give her his hand.

GERALD: I saw you before.

ANABEL: Yes, I know you did.

JOB ARTHUR has disappeared. The men disperse sheepishly into groups, to stand and sit on their heels by the walls and the causeway edge. WILLIE HOUGHTON begins to talk to individuals.

OLIVER: Won't you get in and drive on with us a little way?

ANABEL: No, I was going to church.

OLIVER: Going to church! Is that a new habit?

ANABEL: Not a habit. But I've been twice since I saw you last.

OLIVER: I see. And that's nearly two years ago. It's an annual thing, like a birthday?

ANABEL: No. I'll go on, then.

OLIVER: You'll be late now.

ANABEL: Shall I? It doesn't matter.

OLIVER: We are going to see you again, aren't we?

ANABEL (after a pause): Yes, I hope so, Oliver.

OLIVER: How have you been these two years, well? happy?

ANABEL: No, neither. How have you?

OLIVER: Yes, fairly happy. Have you been ill?

ANABEL: Yes, in France I was very ill.

OLIVER: Your old neuritis?

ANABEL: No. My chest. Pneumonia, oh, a complication.

OLIVER: How sickening! Who looked after you? Is it better?

ANABEL: Yes, it's a great deal better.

OLIVER: And what are you doing in England, working?

ANABEL: No, not much. I won't keep the car here: good-bye.

GERALD: Oh, it's alright.

OLIVER: But, Anabel, we must fix a meeting. I say, wait just a moment. Could I call on your people? Go into town with me one day. I don't know whether Gerald intends to see you, whether he intends to ask you to Lilley Close.

GERALD: I -

ANABEL: He's no need. I'm fixed up there already.

GERALD: What do you mean?

ANABEL: I am at Lilley Close every day, or most days, to work with your sister Winifred in the studio.

GERALD: What? why, how's that?

ANABEL: Your father asked me. My father was already giving her some lessons.

GERALD: And you're at our house every day?

ANABEL: Most days.

GERALD: Well, I'm, well, I'll be, you managed it very sharp, didn't you? I've only been away a fortnight.

ANABEL: Your father asked me, he offered me twelve pounds a month, I wanted to do something.

GERALD: Oh yes, but you didn't hire yourself out at Lilley Close as a sort of upper servant just for twelve pounds a month.

ANABEL: You're wrong, you're wrong. I'm not a sort of upper servant at all, not at all.

GERALD: Oh yes, you are, if you're paid twelve pounds a month, three pounds a week. That's about what Father's sick-nurse gets, I believe. You're a kind of upper servant, like a nurse. You don't do it for twelve pounds a month. You can make twelve pounds in a day, if you like to work at your little models: I know you can sell your little statuette things as soon as you make them.

ANABEL: But I can't make them. I can't make them. I've lost the spirit, the joie de vivre, I don't know what, since I've been ill. I tell you I've got to earn something.

GERALD: Nevertheless, you won't make me believe, Anabel, that you've come and buried yourself in the provinces, such provinces, just to earn Father's three pounds a week. Why don't you admit it, that you came back to try and take up the old threads?

OLIVER: Why not, Gerald? Don't you think we ought to take up the old threads?

GERALD: I don't think we ought to be left without choice. I don't think Anabel ought to come back and thrust herself on me, for that's what it amounts to, after all, when one remembers what's gone before.

ANABEL: I don't thrust myself on you at all. I know I'm a fool, a fool, to come back. But I wanted to. I wanted to see you again. Now I know I've presumed. I've made myself cheap to you. I wanted to, I wanted to. And now I've done it, I won't come to Lilley Close again, nor anywhere where you are. Tell your father I have gone to France again, it will be true.

GERALD: You play tricks on me, and on yourself. You know you do. You do it for the pure enjoyment of it. You're making a scene here in this filthy market-place, just for the fun of it. You like to see these accursed colliers standing eyeing you, and squatting on their heels. You like to catch me out, here where I'm known, where I've been the object of their eyes since I was born. This is a great coup de main for you. I knew it the moment I saw you here.

OLIVER: After all, we are making a scene in the market-place. Get in, Anabel, and we'll settle the dispute more privately. I'm glad you came back, anyhow. I'm glad you came right down on us. Get in, and let us run down to Whatmore.

ANABEL: No, Oliver. I don't want to run down to Whatmore. I wanted to see you, I wanted to see Gerald, and I've seen him, and I've heard him. That will suffice me. We'll make an end of the scene in the market-place. (She turns away.)

OLIVER: I knew it wasn't ended. I knew she would come back and tell us she'd come. But she's done her bit, now she'll go again. My God, what a fool of a world! You go on, Gerald, I'll just go after her and see it out. (Calls.)One moment, Anabel.

ANABEL (calling): Don't come, Oliver. (Turns.)

GERALD: Anabel! (Blows the horn of the motor car violently and agitatedly, she looks round, turns again as if frightened.) God damn the woman! (Gets down from the car.) Drive home for me, Oliver.

CURTAIN

SCENE II

WINIFRED'S studio at Lilley Close. ANABEL and WINIFRED working at a model in clay.

WINIFRED: But isn't it lovely to be in Paris, and to have exhibitions, and to be famous?

ANABEL: Paris was a good place. But I was never famous.

WINIFRED: But your little animals and birds were famous. Jack said so. You know he brought us that bronze thrush that is singing, that is in his room. He has only let me see it twice. It's the loveliest thing I've ever seen. Oh, if I can do anything like that! I've worshipped it, I have. Is it your best thing?

ANABEL: One of the best.

WINIFRED: It must be. When I see it, with its beak lifted, singing, something comes loose in my heart, and I feel as if I should cry, and fly up to heaven. Do you know what I mean? Oh, I'm sure you do, or you could never have made that thrush. Father is so glad you've come to show me how to work. He says now I shall have a life-work, and I shall be happy. It's true, too.

ANABEL: Yes, till the life-work collapses.

WINIFRED: Oh, it can't collapse. I can't believe it could collapse. Do tell me about something else you made, which you loved, something you sculpted. Oh, it makes my heart burn to hear you! Do you think I might call you Anabel? I should love to. You do call me Winifred already.

ANABEL: Yes, do.

WINIFRED: Won't you tell me about something else you made, something lovely?

ANABEL: Well, I did a small kitten, asleep, with its paws crossed. You know, Winifred, that wonderful look that kittens have, as if they were blown along like a bit of fluff, as if they weighed nothing at all, just wafted about, and yet so alive, do you know?

WINIFRED: Darlings, darlings, I love them!

ANABEL: Well, my kitten really came off, it had that quality. It looked as if it had just wafted there.

WINIFRED: Oh, yes! oh, I know! And was it in clay?

ANABEL: I cut it in soft grey stone as well. I loved my kitten. An Armenian bought her.

WINIFRED: And where is she now?

ANABEL: I don't know, in Armenia, I suppose, if there is such a place. It would have to be kept under glass, because the stone wouldn't polish, and I didn't want it polished. But I dislike things under glass, don't you?

WINIFRED: Yes, I do. We had a golden clock, but Gerald wouldn't have the glass cover, and Daddy wouldn't have it without. So now the clock is in Father's room. Gerald often went to Paris. Oliver used to have a studio there. I don't care much for painting, do you?

ANABEL: No. I want something I can touch, if it's something outside me.

WINIFRED: Yes, isn't it wonderful, when things are substantial. Gerald and Oliver came back yesterday from Yorkshire. You know we have a colliery there.

ANABEL: Yes, I believe I've heard.

WINIFRED: I want to introduce you to Gerald, to see if you like him. He's good at the bottom, but he's very overbearing and definite.

ANABEL: Is he?

WINIFRED: Terribly clever in business. He'll get awfully rich.

ANABEL: Isn't he rich enough already?

WINIFRED: Oh yes, because Daddy is rich enough, really. I think if Gerald was a bit different, he'd be really nice. Now he's so managing. It's sickening. Do you dislike managing people, Anabel?

ANABEL: I dislike them extremely, Winifred.

WINIFRED: They're such a bore.

ANABEL: What does Gerald manage?

WINIFRED: Everything. You know he's revolutionized the collieries and the whole Company. He's made a whole new thing of it, so modern. Father says he almost wishes he'd let it die out, let the pits be closed. But I suppose things must be modernized, don't you think? Though it's very unpeaceful, you know, really.

ANABEL: Decidedly unpeaceful, I should say.

WINIFRED: The colliers work awfully hard. The pits are quite wonderful now. Father says it's against nature, all this electricity and so on. Gerald adores electricity. Isn't it curious?

ANABEL: Very. How are you getting on?

WINIFRED: I don't know. It's so hard to make things balance as if they were alive. Where is the balance in a thing that's alive?

ANABEL: The poise? Yes, Winifred, to me, all the secret of life is in that, just the, the inexpressible poise of a living thing, that makes it so different from a dead thing. To me it's the soul, you know, all living things have it, flowers, trees as well. It makes life always marvellous.

WINIFRED: Ah, yes! ah, yes! If only I could put it in my model.

ANABEL: I think you will. You are a sculptor, Winifred. Isn't there someone there?

WINIFRED (running to the door): Oh, Oliver!

OLIVER: Hello, Winnie! Can I come in? This is your sanctum: you can keep us out if you like.

WINIFRED: Oh, no. Do you know Miss Wrath, Oliver? She's a famous sculptress.

OLIVER: Is she? We have met. Is Winifred going to make a sculptress, do you think?

ANABEL: I do.

OLIVER: Good! I like your studio, Winnie. Awfully nice up here over the out-buildings. Are you happy in it?

WINIFRED: Yes, I'm perfectly happy, only I shall never be able to make real models, Oliver, it's so difficult.

OLIVER: Fine room for a party, give us a studio party one day, Win, and we'll dance.

WINIFRED (flying to him): Yes, Oliver, do let us dance. What shall we dance to?

OLIVER: Dance? Dance Vigni-vignons, we all know that. Ready?

WINIFRED: Yes.

They begin to sing, dancing meanwhile, in a free little ballet-manner, a wine-dance, dancing separate and then together.

De terre en vigne
La voilà la jolie vigne,
Vigni-vignons, vignons le vin,
La voilà la jolie vigne au vin,
La voilà la jolie vigne.

OLIVER: Join in, join in, all.

ANABEL joins in; the three dance and move in rhythm.

WINIFRED: I love it, I love it! Do Ma capote à trois boutons, you know it, don't you, Anabel? Ready, now

They begin to dance to a quick little march-rhythm, all singing and dancing till they are out of breath.

OLIVER: Oh! tired! let us sit down.

WINIFRED: Oliver! oh, Oliver! I love you and Anabel.

OLIVER: Oh, Winifred, I brought you a present, you'll love me more now.

WINIFRED: Yes, I shall. Do give it me.

OLIVER: I left it in the morning-room. I put it on the mantelpiece for you.

WINIFRED: Shall I go for it?

OLIVER: There it is, if you want it.

WINIFRED: Yes, do you mind? I won't be long.

WINIFRED goes out.

OLIVER: She's a nice child.

ANABEL: A very nice child.

OLIVER: Why did you come back, Anabel?

ANABEL: Why does the moon rise, Oliver?

OLIVER: For some mischief or other, so they say.

ANABEL: You think I came back for mischief's sake?

OLIVER: Did you?

ANABEL: No.

OLIVER: Ah!

ANABEL: Tell me, Oliver, how is everything now? how is it with you? how is it between us all?

OLIVER: How is it between us all? How isn't it, is more the mark.

ANABEL: Why?

OLIVER: You made a fool of us.

ANABEL: Of whom?

OLIVER: Well, of Gerald particularly, and of me.

ANABEL: How did I make a fool of you, Oliver?

OLIVER: That you know best, Anabel.

ANABEL: No, I don't know. Was it ever right between Gerald and me, all the three years we knew each other, we were together?

OLIVER: Was it all wrong?

ANABEL: No, not all. But it was terrible. It was terrible, Oliver. You don't realize. You don't realize how awful passion can be, when it never resolves, when it never becomes anything else. It is hate, really.

OLIVER: What did you want the passion to resolve into?

ANABEL: I was blinded, maddened. Gerald stung me and stung me till I was mad. I left him for reason's sake, for sanity's sake. We should have killed one another.

OLIVER: You stung him too, you know, and pretty badly, at the last: you dehumanized him.

ANABEL: When? When I left him, you mean?

OLIVER: Yes, when you went away with that Norwegian, playing your game a little too far.

ANABEL: Yes, I knew you'd blame me. I knew you'd be against me. But don't you see, Oliver, you helped to make it impossible for us.

OLIVER: Did I? I didn't intend to.

ANABEL: Ha, ha, Oliver! Your good intentions! They are too good to bear investigation, my friend. Ah, but for your good and friendly intentions

OLIVER: You might have been alright?

ANABEL: No, no, I don't mean that. But we were a vicious triangle, Oliver, you must admit it.

OLIVER: You mean my friendship with Gerald went against you?

ANABEL: Yes. And your friendship with me went against Gerald.

OLIVER: So I am the devil in the piece.

ANABEL: You see, Oliver, Gerald loved you far too well ever to love me altogether. He loved us both. But the Gerald that loved you so dearly, old, old friends as you were, and trusted you, he turned a terrible face of contempt on me. You don't know, Oliver, the cold edge of Gerald's contempt for me, because he was so secure and strong in his old friendship with you. You don't know his sneering attitude to me in the deepest things, because he shared the deepest things with you. He had a passion for me. But he loved you.

OLIVER: Well, he doesn't any more. We went apart after you had gone. The friendship has become almost casual.

ANABEL: You see how bitterly you speak.

OLIVER: Yet you didn't hate me, Anabel.

ANABEL: No, Oliver, I was awfully fond of you. I trusted you, and I trust you still. You see I knew how fond Gerald was of you. And I had to respect this feeling. So I had to be aware of you: I had to be conscious of you: in a way, I had to love you. You understand how I mean? Not with the same fearful love with which I loved Gerald. You seemed to me warm and protecting, like a brother, you know, but a brother one loves.

OLIVER: And then you hated me?

ANABEL: Yes, I had to hate you.

OLIVER: And you hated Gerald?

ANABEL: Almost to madness, almost to madness.

OLIVER: Then you went away with that Norwegian. What of him?

ANABEL: What of him? Well, he's dead.

OLIVER: Ah! That's why you came back?

ANABEL: No, no. I came back because my only hope in life was in coming back. Baard was beautiful, and awful. You know how glisteningly blond he was. Oliver, have you ever watched the polar bears? He was cold as iron when it is so cold that it burns you. Coldness wasn't negative with him. It was positive, and awful beyond expression, like the aurora borealis.

OLIVER: I wonder you ever got back.

ANABEL: Yes, so do I. I feel as if I'd fallen down a fissure in the ice. Yet I have come back, haven't I?

OLIVER: God knows! At least, Anabel, we've gone through too much ever to start the old game again. There'll be no more sticky love between us.

ANABEL: No, I think there won't, either.

OLIVER: And what of Gerald?

ANABEL: I don't know. What do you think of him?

OLIVER: I can't think any more. I can only blindly go from day to day, now.

ANABEL: So can I. Do you think I was wrong to come back? Do you think I wrong Gerald?

OLIVER: No. I'm glad you came. But I feel I can't know anything. We must just go on.

ANABEL: Sometimes I feel I ought never to have come to Gerald again, never, never, never.

OLIVER: Just left the gap? Perhaps, if everything has to come asunder. But I think, if ever there is to be life, hope, then you had to come back. I always knew it. There is something eternal between you and him; and if there is to be any happiness, it depends on that. But perhaps there is to be no more happiness, for our part of the world.

ANABEL (after a pause): Yet I feel hope, don't you?

OLIVER: Yes, sometimes.

ANABEL: It seemed to me, especially that winter in Norway, I can hardly express it, as if any moment life might give way under one, like thin ice, and one would be more than dead. And then I knew my only hope was here, the only hope.

OLIVER: Yes, I believe it. And I believe

Enter MRS BARLOW.

MRS BARLOW: Oh, I wanted to speak to you, Oliver.

OLIVER: Shall I come across?

MRS BARLOW: No, not now. I believe Father is coming here with Gerald.

OLIVER: Is he going to walk so far?

MRS BARLOW: He will do it. I suppose you know Oliver?

ANABEL: Yes, we have met before.

MRS BARLOW (to OLIVER): You didn't mention it. Where have you met Miss Wrath? She's been about the world, I believe.

ANABEL: About the world? no, Mrs Barlow. If one happens to know Paris and London

MRS BARLOW: Paris and London! Well, I don't say you are altogether an adventuress. My husband seems very pleased with you, for Winifred's sake, I suppose, and he's wrapped up in Winifred.

ANABEL: Winifred is an artist.

MRS BARLOW: All my children have the artist in them. They get it from my family. My father went mad in Rome. My family is born with a black fate, they all inherit it.

OLIVER: I believe one is master of one's fate sometimes, Mrs Barlow. There are moments of pure choice.

MRS BARLOW: Between two ways to the same end, no doubt. There's no changing the end.

OLIVER: I think there is.

MRS BARLOW: Yes, you have a parvenu's presumptuousness somewhere about you.

OLIVER: Well, better than a blue-blooded fatalism.

MRS BARLOW: The fate is in the blood: you can't change the blood.

Enter WINIFRED.

WINIFRED: Oh, thank you, Oliver, for the wolf and the goat, thank you so much! The wolf has sprung on the goat, Miss Wrath, and has her by the throat.

ANABEL: The wolf?

OLIVER: It's a little marble group, Italian, in hard marble.

WINIFRED: The wolf, I love the wolf, he pounces so beautifully. His backbone is so terribly fierce. I don't feel a bit sorry for the goat, somehow.

OLIVER: I didn't. She is too much like the wrong sort of clergyman.

WINIFRED: Yes, such a stiff, long face. I wish he'd kill her.

MRS BARLOW: There's a wish!

WINIFRED: Father and Gerald are coming. That's them, I suppose.

Enter MR BARLOW and GERALD.

MR BARLOW: Ah, good morning, good morning, quite a little gathering! Ah

OLIVER: The steps tire you, Mr Barlow.

MR BARLOW: A little, a little, thank you. Well, Miss Wrath, are you quite comfortable here?

ANABEL: Very comfortable, thanks.

GERALD: It was clever of you, Father, to turn this place into a studio.

MR BARLOW: Yes, Gerald. You make the worldly schemes and I the homely. Yes, it's a delightful place. I shall come here often if the two young ladies will allow me. By the way, Miss Wrath, I don't know if you have been introduced to my son Gerald. I beg your pardon. Miss Wrath, Gerald, my son, Miss Wrath. (They bow.) Well, we are quite a gathering, quite a pleasant little gathering. We never expected anything so delightful a month ago, did we, Winifred, darling?

WINIFRED: No, Daddy, it's much nicer than expectations.

MR BARLOW: So it is, dear, to have such exceptional companionship and such a pleasant retreat. We are very happy to have Miss Wrath with us, very happy.

GERALD: A studio's awfully nice, you know; it is such a retreat. A newspaper has no effect in it, falls quite flat, no matter what the headlines are.

MR BARLOW: Quite true, Gerald, dear. It is a sanctum the world cannot invade, unlike all other sanctuaries, I am afraid.

GERALD: By the way, Oliver, to go back to profanities, the colliers really are coming out in support of the poor, ill-used clerks.

MR BARLOW: No, no, Gerald, no, no! Don't be such an alarmist. Let us leave these subjects before the ladies. No, no: the clerks will have their increase quite peacefully.

GERALD: Yes, dear father, but they can't have it peacefully now. We've been threatened already by the colliers, we've already received an ultimatum.

MR BARLOW: Nonsense, my boy, nonsense! Don't let us split words. You won't go against the clerks in such a small matter. Always avoid trouble over small matters. Don't make bad feeling, don't make bad blood.

MRS BARLOW: The blood is already rotten in this neighbourhood. What it needs is letting out. We need a few veins opening, or we shall have mortification setting in. The blood is black.

MR BARLOW: We won't accept your figure of speech literally, dear. No, Gerald, don't go to war over trifles.

GERALD: It's just over trifles that one must make war, Father. One can yield gracefully over big matters. But to be bullied over trifles is a sign of criminal weakness.

MR BARLOW: Ah, not so, not so, my boy. When you are as old as I am, you will know the comparative insignificance of these trifles.

GERALD: The older I get, Father, the more such trifles stick in my throat.

MR BARLOW: Ah, it is an increasingly irritable disposition in you, my child. Nothing costs so bitterly, in the end, as a stubborn pride.

MRS BARLOW: Except a stubborn humility, and that will cost you more. Avoid humility, beware of stubborn humility: it degrades. Hark, Gerald, fight! When the occasion comes, fight! If it's one against five thousand, fight! Don't give them your heart on a dish! Never! If they want to eat your heart out, make them fight for it, and then give it them poisoned at last, poisoned with your own blood. What do you say, young woman?

ANABEL: Is it for me to speak, Mrs Barlow?

MRS BARLOW: Weren't you asked?

ANABEL: Certainly I would never give the world my heart on a dish. But can't there ever be peace, real peace?

MRS BARLOW: No, not while there is devilish enmity.

MR BARLOW: You are wrong, dear, you are wrong. The peace can come, the peace that passeth all understanding.

MRS BARLOW: That there is already between me and Almighty God. I am at peace with the God that made me, and made me proud. With men who humiliate me I am at war. Between me and the shameful humble there is war to the end, though they are millions and I am one. I hate the people. Between my race and them there is war, between them and me, between them and my children, for ever war, for ever and ever.

MR BARLOW: Ah, Henrietta, you have said all this before.

MRS BARLOW: And say it again. Fight, Gerald. You have my blood in you, thank God. Fight for it, Gerald. Spend it as if it were costly, Gerald, drop by drop. Let no dogs lap it. Look at your father. He set his heart on a plate at the door, for the poorest mongrel to eat up. See him now, wasted and crossed out like a mistake, and swear, Gerald, swear to be true to my blood in you. Never lie down before the mob, Gerald. Fight it and stab it, and die fighting. It's a lost hope, but fight!

GERALD: Don't say these things here, Mother.

MRS BARLOW: Yes, I will, I will. I'll say them before you, and the child Winifred, she knows. And before Oliver and the young woman, they know, too.

MR BARLOW: You see, dear, you can never understand that, although I am weak and wasted, although I may be crossed out from the world like a mistake, I still have peace in my soul, dear, the peace that passeth all understanding.

MRS BARLOW: And what right have you to it? All very well for you to take peace with you into the other world. What do you leave for your sons to inherit?

MR BARLOW: The peace of God, Henrietta, if there is no peace among men.

MRS BARLOW: Then why did you have children? Why weren't you celibate? They have to live among men. If they have no place among men, why have you put them there? If the peace of God is no more than the peace of death, why are your sons born of you? How can you have peace with God, if you leave no peace for your sons, no peace, no pride, no place on earth?

GERALD: Nay, Mother, nay. You shall never blame Father on my behalf.

MRS BARLOW: Don't trouble, he is blameless, I, a hulking, half-demented woman, I am glad when you blame me. But don't blame me when I tell you to fight. Don't do that, or you will regret it when you must die. Ah, your father was stiff and proud enough before men of better rank than himself. He was overbearing enough with his equals and his betters. But he humbled himself before the poor, he made me ashamed. He must hear it, he must hear it! Better he should hear it than die coddling himself with peace. His humility, and my pride, they have made a nice ruin of each other. Yet he is the man I wanted to marry, he is the man I would marry again. But never, never again would I give way before his goodness. Gerald, if you must be true to your father, be true to me as well. Don't set me down at nothing because I haven't a humble case.

GERALD: No, Mother, no, dear Mother. You see, dear Mother, I have rather a job between the two halves of myself. When you come to have the wild horses in your own soul, Mother, it makes it difficult.

MRS BARLOW: Never mind, you'll have help.

GERALD: Thank you for the assurance, darling. Father, you don't mind what Mother says, I hope. I believe there's some truth in it, don't you?

MR BARLOW: I have nothing to say.

WINIFRED: I think there's some truth in it, Daddy. You were always worrying about those horrid colliers, and they didn't care a bit about you. And they ought to have cared a million pounds.

MR BARLOW: You don't understand, my child.

CURTAIN

ACT II

SCENE: Evening of the same day. Drawing-room at Lilley Close. MR BARLOW, GERALD, WINIFRED, ANABEL, OLIVER present. BUTLER pours coffee.

MR BARLOW: And you are quite a stranger in these parts, Miss Wrath?

ANABEL: Practically. But I was born at Derby.

MR BARLOW: I was born in this house, but it was a different affair then: my father was a farmer, you know. The coal has brought us what moderate wealth we have. Of course, we were never poor or needy, farmers, substantial farmers. And I think we were happier so, yes. Winnie, dear, hand Miss Wrath the sweets. I hope they're good. I ordered them from London for you. Oliver, my boy, have you everything you like? That's right. It gives me such pleasure to see a little festive gathering in this room again. I wish Bertie and Elinor might be here. What time is it, Gerald?

GERALD: A quarter to nine, Father.

MR BARLOW: Not late yet. I can sit with you another half-hour. I am feeling better to-day. Winifred, sing something to us.

WINIFRED: Something jolly, Father?

MR BARLOW: Very jolly, darling.

WINIFRED: I'll sing "The Lincolnshire Poacher", shall I?

MR BARLOW: Do, darling, and we'll all join in the chorus. Will you join in the chorus, Miss Wrath?

ANABEL: I will. It is a good song.

MR BARLOW: Yes, isn't it!

WINIFRED: All dance for the chorus, as well as singing.

They sing; some pirouette a little for the chorus.

MR BARLOW: Ah, splendid, splendid! There is nothing like gaiety.

WINIFRED: I do love to dance about. I know: let us do a little ballet, four of us, oh, do!

GERALD: What ballet, Winifred?

WINIFRED: Any. Eva can play for us. She plays well.

MR BARLOW: You won't disturb your mother? Don't disturb Eva if she is busy with your mother.

Exit WINIFRED.

If only I can see Winifred happy, my heart is at rest: if only I can hope for her to be happy in her life.

GERALD: Oh, Winnie's alright, Father, especially now she has Miss Wrath to initiate her into the mysteries of life and labour.

ANABEL: Why are you ironical?

MR BARLOW: Oh, Miss Wrath, believe me, we all feel that, it is the greatest possible pleasure to me that you have come.

GERALD: I wasn't ironical, I assure you.

MR BARLOW: No, indeed, no, indeed! We have every belief in you.

ANABEL: But why should you have?

MR BARLOW: Ah, my dear child, allow us the credit of our own discernment. And don't take offence at my familiarity. I am afraid I am spoilt since I am an invalid.

Re-enter WINIFRED, with EVA.

MR BARLOW: Come, Eva, you will excuse us for upsetting your evening. Will you be so good as to play something for us to dance to?

EVA: Yes, sir. What shall I play?

WINIFRED: Mozart, I'll find you the piece. Mozart's the saddest musician in the world, but he's the best to dance to.

MR BARLOW: Why, how is it you are such a connoisseur in sadness, darling?

GERALD: She isn't. She's a flagrant amateur.

EVA plays; they dance a little ballet.

MR BARLOW: Charming, charming, Miss Wrath: will you allow me to say Anabel, we shall all feel so much more at home? Yes, thank you, er, you enter into the spirit of it wonderfully, Anabel, dear. The others are accustomed to play together. But it is not so easy to come in on occasion as you do.

GERALD: Oh, Anabel's a genius! I beg your pardon, Miss Wrath, familiarity is catching.

MR BARLOW: Gerald, my boy, don't forget that you are virtually host here.

EVA: Did you want any more music, sir?

GERALD: No, don't stay, Eva. We mustn't tire Father.

Exit EVA.

MR BARLOW: I am afraid, Anabel, you will have a great deal to excuse in us, in the way of manners. We have never been a formal household. But you have lived in the world of artists: you will understand, I hope.

ANABEL: Oh, surely

MR BARLOW: Yes, I know. We have been a turbulent family, and we have had our share of sorrow, even more, perhaps, than of joys. And sorrow makes one indifferent to the conventionalities of life.

GERALD: Excuse me, Father: do you mind if I go and write a letter I have on my conscience?

MR BARLOW: No, my boy. (Exit GERALD.) We have had our share of sorrow and of conflict, Miss Wrath, as you may have gathered.

ANABEL: Yes, a little.

MR BARLOW: The mines were opened when my father was a boy, the first, and I was born late, when he was nearly fifty. So that all my life has been involved with coal and colliers. As a young man, I was gay and thoughtless. But I married young, and we lost our first child through a terrible accident. Two children we have lost through sudden and violent death. (WINIFRED goes out unnoticed.) It made me reflect. And when I came to reflect, Anabel, I could not justify my position in life. If I believed in the teachings of the New Testament, which I did, and do, how could I keep two or three thousand men employed underground in the mines, at a wage, let us say, of two pounds a week, whilst I lived in this comfortable house, and took something like two thousand pounds a year, let us name any figure

ANABEL: Yes, of course. But is it money that really matters, Mr Barlow?

MR BARLOW: My dear, if you are a working man, it matters. When I went into the homes of my poor fellows, when they were ill or had had accidents, then I knew it mattered. I knew that the great disparity was wrong, even as we are taught that it is wrong.

ANABEL: Yes, I believe that the great disparity is a mistake. But take their lives, Mr Barlow. Do you think they would live more, if they had more money? Do you think the poor live less than the rich? is their life emptier?

MR BARLOW: Surely their lives would be better, Anabel.

OLIVER: All our lives would be better, if we hadn't to hang on in the perpetual tug-of-war, like two donkeys pulling at one carrot. The ghastly tension of possessions, and struggling for possession, spoils life for everybody.

MR BARLOW: Yes, I know now, as I knew then, that it was wrong. But how to avoid the wrong? If I gave away the whole of my income, it would merely be an arbitrary dispensation of charity. The money would still be mine to give, and those that received it would probably only be weakened instead of strengthened. And then my wife was accustomed to a certain way of living, a certain establishment. Had I any right to sacrifice her, without her consent?

ANABEL: Why, no!

MR BARLOW: Again, if I withdrew from the Company, if I retired on a small income, I knew that another man would automatically take my place, and make it probably harder for the men.

ANABEL: Of course, while the system stands, if one makes self-sacrifice one only panders to the system, makes it fatter.

MR BARLOW: One panders to the system, one panders to the system. And so, you see, the problem is too much. One man cannot alter or affect the system; he can only sacrifice himself to it. Which is the worst thing probably that he can do.

OLIVER: Quite. But why feel guilty for the system? everybody supports it, the poor as much as the rich. If every rich man withdrew from the system, the working classes and socialists would keep it going, every man in the hope of getting rich himself at last. It's the people that are wrong. They want the system much more than the rich do, because they are much more anxious to be rich, never having been rich, poor devils.

MR BARLOW: Just the system. So I decided at last that the best way was to give every private help that lay in my power. I would help my men individually and personally, wherever I could. Not one of them came to me and went away unheard; and there was no distress which could be alleviated that I did not try to alleviate. Yet I am afraid that the greatest distress I never heard of, the most distressed never came to me. They hid their trouble.

ANABEL: Yes, the decent ones.

MR BARLOW: But I wished to help, it was my duty. Still, I think that, on the whole, we were a comfortable and happy community. Barlow and Walsall's men were not unhappy in those days, I believe. We were liberal; the men lived.

OLIVER: Yes, that is true. Even twenty years ago the place was still jolly.

MR BARLOW: And then, when Gerald was a lad of thirteen, came the great lock-out. We belonged to the Masters' Federation, I was but one man on the Board. We had to abide by the decision. The mines were closed till the men would accept the reduction. Well, that cut my life across. We were shutting the men out from work, starving their families, in order to force them to accept a reduction. It may be the condition of trade made it imperative. But, for myself, I would rather have lost everything. Of course, we did what we could. Food was very cheap, practically given away. We had open kitchen here. And it was mercifully warm summer-time. Nevertheless, there was privation and suffering, and trouble and bitterness. We had the redcoats down, even to guard this house. And from this window I saw Whatmore head-stocks ablaze, and before I could get to the spot the soldiers had shot two poor fellows. They were not killed, thank God

OLIVER: Ah, but they enjoyed it, they enjoyed it immensely. I remember what grand old sporting weeks they were. It was like a fox-hunt, so lively and gay, bands and tea-parties and excitement everywhere, pit-ponies loose, men all over the countryside

MR BARLOW: There was a great deal of suffering which you were too young to appreciate. However, since that year I have had to acknowledge a new situation, a radical if unspoken opposition between masters and men. Since that year we have been split into opposite camps. Whatever I might privately feel, I was one of the owners, one of the masters, and therefore in the opposite camp. To my men I was an oppressor, a representative of injustice and greed. Privately, I like to think that even to this day they bear me no malice, that they have some lingering regard for me. But the master stands before the human being, and the condition of war overrides individuals, they hate the master, even whilst, as a human being, he would be their friend. I recognize the inevitable justice. It is the price one has to pay.

ANABEL: Yes, it is difficult, very.

MR BARLOW: Perhaps I weary you?

ANABEL: Oh, no, no.

MR BARLOW: Well, then the mines began to pay badly. The seams ran thin and unprofitable, work was short. Either we must close down or introduce a new system, American methods, which I dislike so extremely. Now it really became a case of men working against machines, flesh and blood working against iron, for a livelihood. Still, it had to be done, the whole system revolutionized. Gerald took it in hand, and now I hardly know my own pits, with the great electric plants and strange machinery, and the new coal-cutters, iron men, as the colliers call them, everything running at top speed, utterly dehumanized, inhuman. Well, it had to be done; it was the only alternative to closing down and throwing three thousand men out of work. And Gerald has done it. But I can't bear to see it. The men of this generation are not like my men. They are worn and gloomy; they have a hollow look that I can't bear to see. They are a great grief to me. I remember my men even twenty years ago, a noisy, lively, careless set, who kept the place ringing. Now it is too quiet, too quiet. There is something wrong in the quietness, something unnatural. I feel it is unnatural; I feel afraid of it. And I cannot help feeling guilty.

ANABEL: Yes, I understand. It terrifies me.

MR BARLOW: Does it? does it? Yes. And as my wife says, I leave it all to Gerald, this terrible situation. But I appeal to God, if anything in my power could have averted it, I would have averted it. I would have made any sacrifice. For it is a great and bitter trouble to me.

ANABEL: Ah, well, in death there is no industrial situation. Something must be different there.

MR BARLOW: Yes, yes.

OLIVER: And you see sacrifice isn't the slightest use. If only people would be sane and decent.

MR BARLOW: Yes, indeed. Would you be so good as to ring, Oliver? I think I must go to bed.

ANABEL: Ah, you have over-tired yourself.

MR BARLOW: No, my dear, not over-tired. Excuse me if I have burdened you with all this. It relieves me to speak of it.

ANABEL: I realize how terrible it is, Mr Barlow, and how helpless one is.

MR BARLOW: Thank you, my dear, for your sympathy.

OLIVER: If the people for one minute pulled themselves up and conquered their mania for money and machine excitement, the whole thing would be solved. Would you like me to find Winnie and tell her to say good night to you?

MR BARLOW: If you would be so kind. (Exit OLIVER.) Can't you find a sweet that you would like, my dear? Won't you take a little cherry brandy?

Enter BUTLER.

ANABEL: Thank you.

WILLIAM: You will go up, sir?

MR BARLOW: Yes, William.

WILLIAM: You are tired to-night, sir.

MR BARLOW: It has come over me just now.

WILLIAM: I wish you went up before you became so over-tired, sir. Would you like Nurse?

MR BARLOW: No, I'll go with you, William. Good night, my dear.

ANABEL: Good night, Mr Barlow. I am so sorry if you are overtired.

Exit BUTLER and MR BARLOW. ANABEL takes a drink and goes to the fire. Enter GERALD.

GERALD: Father gone up?

ANABEL: Yes.

GERALD: I thought I heard him. Has he been talking too much? Poor Father, he will take things to heart.

ANABEL: Tragic, really.

GERALD: Yes, I suppose it is. But one can get beyond tragedy, beyond the state of feeling tragical, I mean. Father himself is tragical. One feels he is mistaken, and yet he wouldn't be any different, and be himself, I suppose. He's sort of crucified on an idea of the working people. It's rather horrible when he's one father. However, apart from tragedy, how do you like being here, in this house?

ANABEL: I like the house. It's rather too comfortable.

GERALD: Yes. But how do you like being here?

ANABEL: How do you like my being in your home?

GERALD: Oh, I think you're very decorative.

ANABEL: More decorative than comfortable?

GERALD: Perhaps. But perhaps you give the necessary finish to the establishment.

ANABEL: Like the correct window-curtains?

GERALD: Yes, something like that. I say, why did you come, Anabel? Why did you come slap-bang into the middle of us? It's not expostulation, I want to know.

ANABEL: You mean you want to be told.

GERALD: Yes, I want to be told.

ANABEL: That's rather mean of you. You should savvy, and let it go without saying.

GERALD: Yes, but I don't savvy.

ANABEL: Then wait till you do.

GERALD: No, I want to be told. There's a difference in you, Anabel, that puts me out, rather. You're sort of softer and sweeter, I'm not sure whether it isn't a touch of Father in you. There's a little sanctified smudge on your face. Are you really a bit sanctified?

ANABEL: No, not sanctified. It's true I feel different. I feel I want a new way of life, something more dignified, more religious, if you like, anyhow, something positive.

GERALD: Is it the change of heart, Anabel?

ANABEL: Perhaps it is, Gerald.

GERALD: I'm not sure that I like it. Isn't it like a berry that decides to get very sweet, and goes soft?

ANABEL: I don't think so.

GERALD: Slightly sanctimonious. I think I liked you better before. I don't think I like you with this touch of aureole. People seem to me so horribly self-satisfied when they get a change of heart, they take such a fearful lot of credit to themselves on the strength of it.

ANABEL: I don't think I do. Do you feel no different, Gerald?

GERALD: Radically, I can't say I do. I feel very much more indifferent.

ANABEL: What to?

GERALD: Everything.

ANABEL: You're still angry, that's what it is.

GERALD: Oh yes, I'm angry. But that is part of my normal state.

ANABEL: Why are you angry?

GERALD: Is there any reason why I shouldn't be angry? I'm angry because you treated me, well, so impudently, really, clearing out and leaving one to whistle to the empty walls.

ANABEL: Don't you think it was time I cleared out, when you became so violent, and really dangerous, really like a madman?

GERALD: Time or not time, you went, you disappeared and left us high and dry, and I am still angry. But I'm not only angry about that. I'm angry with the colliers, with Labour for its low-down impudence, and I'm angry with Father for being so ill, and I'm angry with Mother for looking such a hopeless thing, and I'm angry with Oliver because he thinks so much

ANABEL: And what are you angry with yourself for?

GERALD: I'm angry with myself for being myself, I always was that. I was always a curse to myself.

ANABEL: And that's why you curse others so much?

GERALD: You talk as if butter wouldn't melt in your mouth.

ANABEL: You see, Gerald, there has to be a change. You'll have to change.

GERALD: Change of heart? Well, it won't be to get softer, Anabel.

ANABEL: You needn't be softer. But you can be quieter, more sane even. There ought to be some part of you that can be quiet and apart from the world, some part that can be happy and gentle.

GERALD: Well, there isn't. I don't pretend to be able to extricate a soft sort of John Halifax, Gentleman, out of the machine I'm mixed up in, and keep him to gladden the connubial hearth. I'm angry, and I'm angry right through, and I'm not going to play bo-peep with myself, pretending I'm not.

ANABEL: Nobody asks you to. But is there no part of you that can be a bit gentle and peaceful and happy with a woman?

GERALD: No, there isn't. I'm not going to smug with you, no, not I. You're smug in your coming back. You feel virtuous, and expect me to rise to it. I won't.

ANABEL: Then I'd better have stayed away.

GERALD: If you want me to virtue-ize and smug with you, you had.

ANABEL: What do you want, then?

GERALD: I don't know. I know I don't want that.

ANABEL: Oh, very well. (Goes to the piano; begins to play.)

Enter MRS BARLOW.

GERALD: Hello, Mother! Father has gone to bed.

MRS BARLOW: Oh, I thought he was down here talking. You two alone?

GERALD: With the piano for chaperone, Mother.

MRS BARLOW: That's more than I gave you credit for. I haven't come to chaperone you either, Gerald.

GERALD: Chaperone me, Mother! Do you think I need it?

MRS BARLOW: If you do, you won't get it. I've come too late to be of any use in that way, as far as I hear.

GERALD: What have you heard, Mother?

MRS BARLOW: I heard Oliver and this young woman talking.

GERALD: Oh, did you? When? What did they say?

MRS BARLOW: Something about married in the sight of heaven, but couldn't keep it up on earth.

GERALD: I don't understand.

MRS BARLOW: That you and this young woman were married in the sight of heaven, or through eternity, or something similar, but that you couldn't make up your minds to it on earth.

GERALD: Really! That's very curious, Mother.

MRS BARLOW: Very common occurrence, I believe.

GERALD: Yes, so it is. But I don't think you heard quite right, dear. There seems to be some lingering uneasiness in heaven as a matter of fact. We'd quite made up our minds to live apart on earth. But where did you hear this, Mother?

MRS BARLOW: I heard it outside the studio door this morning.

GERALD: You mean you happened to be on one side of the door while Oliver and Anabel were talking on the other?

MRS BARLOW: You'd make a detective, Gerald, you're so good at putting two and two together. I listened till I'd heard as much as I wanted. I'm not sure I didn't come down here hoping to hear another conversation going on.

GERALD: Listen outside the door, darling?

MRS BARLOW: There'd be nothing to listen to if I were inside.

GERALD: It isn't usually done, you know.

MRS BARLOW: I listen outside doors when I have occasion to be interested, which isn't often, unfortunately for me.

GERALD: But I've a queer feeling that you have a permanent occasion to be interested in me. I only half like it.

MRS BARLOW: It's surprising how uninteresting you are, Gerald, for a man of your years. I have not had occasion to listen outside a door, for you, no, not for a great while, believe me.

GERALD: I believe you implicitly, darling. But do you happen to know me through and through, and in and out, all my past and present doings, Mother? Have you a secret access to my room, and a spy-hole, and all those things? This is uncomfortably thrilling. You take on a new lustre.

MRS BARLOW: Your memoirs wouldn't make you famous, my son.

GERALD: Infamous, dear?

MRS BARLOW: Good heavens, no! What a lot you expect from your very mild sins! You and this young woman have lived together, then?

GERALD: Don't say "this young woman", Mother dear, it's slightly vulgar. It isn't for me to compromise Anabel by admitting such a thing, you know.

MRS BARLOW: Do you ask me to call her Anabel? I won't.

GERALD: Then say "this person", Mother. It's more becoming.

MRS BARLOW: I didn't come to speak to you, Gerald. I know you. I came to speak to this young woman.

GERALD: "Person", Mother. Will you curtsey, Anabel? And I'll twist my handkerchief. We shall make a Cruikshank drawing, if Mother makes her hair a little more slovenly.

MRS BARLOW: You and Gerald were together for some time?

GERALD: Three years, off and on, Mother.

MRS BARLOW: And then you suddenly dropped my son, and went away?

GERALD: To Norway, Mother, so I have gathered.

MRS BARLOW: And now you have come back because that last one died?

GERALD: Is he dead, Anabel? How did he die?

ANABEL: He was killed on the ice.

GERALD: Oh, God!

MRS BARLOW: Now, having had your fill of tragedy, you have come back to be demure and to marry Gerald. Does he thank you?

GERALD: You must listen outside the door, Mother, to find that out.

MRS BARLOW: Well, it's your own affair.

GERALD: What a lame summing up, Mother! quite unworthy of you.

ANABEL: What did you wish to say to me, Mrs Barlow? Please say it.

MRS BARLOW: What did I wish to say! Ay, what did I wish to say! What is the use of my saying anything? What am I but a buffoon and a slovenly caricature in the family?

GERALD: No, Mother dear, don't climb down, please don't. Tell Anabel what you wanted to say.

MRS BARLOW: Yes, yes, yes. I came to say, don't be good to my son, don't be good to him.

GERALD: Sounds weak, dear, mere contrariness.

MRS BARLOW: Don't presume to be good to my son, young woman. I won't have it, even if he will. You hear me?

ANABEL: Yes. I won't presume, then.

GERALD: May she presume to be bad to me, Mother?

MRS BARLOW: For that you may look after yourself. But a woman who was good to him would ruin him in six months, take the manhood out of him. He has a tendency, a secret hankering, to make a gift of himself to somebody. He shan't do it. I warn you. I am not a woman to be despised.

ANABEL: No, I understand.

MRS BARLOW: Only one other thing I ask. If he must fight, and fight he must, let him alone: don't you try to shield him or save him. Don't interfere, do you hear?

ANABEL: Not till I must.

MRS BARLOW: Never. Learn your place, and keep it. Keep away from him, if you are going to be a wife to him. Don't go too near. And don't let him come too near. Beat him off if he tries. Keep a solitude in your heart even when you love him best. Keep it. If you lose it, you lose everything.

GERALD: But that isn't love, Mother.

MRS BARLOW: What?

GERALD: That isn't love.

MRS BARLOW: What? What do you know of love, you ninny? You only know the feeding-bottle. It's what you want, all of you, to be brought up by hand, and mew about love. Ah, God! Ah, God! that you should none of you know the only thing which would make you worth having.

GERALD: I don't believe in your only thing, Mother. But what is it?

MRS BARLOW: What you haven't got, the power to be alone.

GERALD: Sort of megalomania, you mean?

MRS BARLOW: What? Megalomania! What is your love but a megalomania, flowing over everybody, and everything like spilt water? Megalomania! I hate you, you softy! I would beat you (suddenly advancing on him and beating him fiercely) beat you into some manhood, beat you

GERALD: Stop, Mother, keep off.

MRS BARLOW: It's the men who need beating nowadays, not the children. Beat the softness out of him, young woman. It's the only way, if you love him enough, if you love him enough.

GERALD: You hear, Anabel?

Speak roughly to your little boy,
And beat him when he sneezes.

MRS BARLOW (catching up a large old fan, and smashing it about his head): You softy, you piffler, you will never have had enough! Ah, you should be thrust in the fire, you should, to have the softness and the brittleness burnt out of you!

The door opens, OLIVER TURTON enters, followed by JOB ARTHUR FREER. MRS BARLOW is still attacking GERALD. She turns, infuriated.

Go out! Go out! What do you mean by coming in unannounced? Take him upstairs, take that fellow into the library, Oliver Turton.

GERALD: Mother, you improve our already pretty reputation. Already they say you are mad.

MRS BARLOW (ringing violently): Let me be mad then. I am mad, driven mad. One day I shall kill you, Gerald.

GERALD: You won't, Mother, because I shan't let you.

MRS BARLOW: Let me! let me! As if I should wait for you to let me!

GERALD: I am a match for you even in violence, come to that.

MRS BARLOW: A match! A damp match. A wet match.

Enter BUTLER.

WILLIAM: You rang, madam?

MRS BARLOW: Clear up those bits. Where are you going to see that white-faced fellow? Here?

GERALD: I think so.

MRS BARLOW: You will still have them coming to the house, will you? You will still let them trample in our private rooms, will you? Bah! I ought to leave you to your own devices.

Exit MRS BARLOW.

GERALD: When you've done that, William, ask Mr Freer to come down here.

WILLIAM: Yes, sir.

A pause. Exit WILLIAM.

GERALD: So, o-o. You've had another glimpse of the family life.

ANABEL: Yes. Rather disturbing.

GERALD: Not at all, when you're used to it. Mother isn't as mad as she pretends to be.

ANABEL: I don't think she's mad at all. I think she has most desperate courage.

GERALD: "Courage" is good. That's a new term for it.

ANABEL: Yes, courage. When a man says "courage" he means the courage to die. A woman means the courage to live. That's what women hate men most for; that they haven't the courage to live.

GERALD: Mother takes her courage into both hands rather late.

ANABEL: We're a little late ourselves.

GERALD: We are, rather. By the way, you seem to have had plenty of the courage of death, you've played a pretty deathly game, it seems to me, both when I knew you and afterwards, you've had your finger pretty deep in the death-pie.

ANABEL: That's why I want a change of, of

GERALD: Of heart? Better take Mother's tip, and try the poker.

ANABEL: I will.

GERALD: Ha, corraggio!

ANABEL: Yes, corraggio!

GERALD: Corraggiaccio!

ANABEL: Corraggione!

GERALD: Cock-a-doodle-doo!

Enter OLIVER and FREER.

Oh, come in. Don't be afraid; it's a charade. (ANABEL rises.) No, don't go, Anabel. Corraggio! Take a seat, Mr Freer.

JOB ARTHUR: Sounds like a sneezing game, doesn't it?

GERALD: It is. Do you know the famous rhyme:

Speak roughly to your little boy,
And beat him when he sneezes?

JOB ARTHUR: No, I can't say I do.

GERALD: My mother does. Will you have anything to drink? Will you help yourself?

JOB ARTHUR: Well, no, I don't think I'll have anything, thanks.

GERALD: A cherry brandy? Yes? ANABEL, what's yours.

ANABEL: Did I see Kümmel?

GERALD: You did. (They all take drinks.) What's the latest, Mr Freer?

JOB ARTHUR: The latest? Well, I don't know, I'm sure

GERALD: Oh, yes. Trot it out. We're quite private.

JOB ARTHUR: Well, I don't know. There's several things.

GERALD: The more the merrier.

JOB ARTHUR: I'm not so sure. The men are in a very funny temper, Mr Barlow, very funny.

GERALD: Coincidence, so am I. Not surprising, is it?

JOB ARTHUR: The men, perhaps not.

GERALD: What else, Job Arthur?

JOB ARTHUR: You know the men have decided to stand by the office men?

GERALD: Yes.

JOB ARTHUR: They've agreed to come out next Monday.

GERALD: Have they?

JOB ARTHUR: Yes; there was no stopping them. They decided for it like one man.

GERALD: How was that?

JOB ARTHUR: That's what surprises me. They're a jolly sight more certain over this than they've ever been over their own interests.

GERALD: All their love for the office clerks coming out in a rush?

JOB ARTHUR: Well, I don't know about love; but that's how it is.

GERALD: What is it, if it isn't love?

JOB ARTHUR: I can't say. They're in a funny temper. It's hard to make out.

GERALD: A funny temper, are they? Then I suppose we ought to laugh.

JOB ARTHUR: No, I don't think it's a laughing matter. They're coming out on Monday for certain.

GERALD: Yes, so are daffodils.

JOB ARTHUR: Beg pardon?

GERALD: Daffodils.

JOB ARTHUR: No, I don't follow what you mean.

GERALD: Don't you? But I thought Alfred Breffitt and William Straw were not very popular.

JOB ARTHUR: No, they aren't, not in themselves. But it's the principle of the thing, so it seems.

GERALD: What principle?

JOB ARTHUR: Why, all sticking together, for one thing, all Barlow and Walsall's men holding by one another.

GERALD: United we stand?

JOB ARTHUR: That's it. And then it's the strong defending the weak as well. There's three thousand colliers standing up for thirty-odd office men. I must say I think it's sporting myself.

GERALD: You do, do you? United we stand, divided we fall. What do they stand for, really? What is it?

JOB ARTHUR: Well, for their right to a living wage. That's how I see it.

GERALD: For their right to a living wage! Just that?

JOB ARTHUR: Yes, sir, that's how I see it.

GERALD: Well, that doesn't seem so preposterously difficult, does it?

JOB ARTHUR: Why, that's what I think myself, Mr Gerald. It's such a little thing.

GERALD: Quite. I suppose the men themselves are to judge what is a living wage?

JOB ARTHUR: Oh, I think they're quite reasonable, you know.

GERALD: Oh, yes, eminently reasonable. Reason's their strong point. And if they get their increase, they'll be quite contented?

JOB ARTHUR: Yes, as far as I know, they will.

GERALD: As far as you know? Why, is there something you don't know? something you're not sure about?

JOB ARTHUR: No, I don't think so. I think they'll be quite satisfied this time.

GERALD: Why this time? Is there going to be a next time, every-day-has-its-to-morrow kind of thing?

JOB ARTHUR: I don't know about that. It's a funny world, Mr Barlow.

GERALD: Yes, I quite believe it. How do you see it funny?

JOB ARTHUR: Oh, I don't know. Everything's in a funny state.

GERALD: What do you mean by everything?

JOB ARTHUR: Well, I mean things in general, Labour, for example.

GERALD: You think Labour's in a funny state, do you? What do you think it wants? What do you think, personally?

JOB ARTHUR: Well, in my own mind, I think it wants a bit of its own back.

GERALD: And how does it mean to get it?

JOB ARTHUR: Ha! that's not so easy to say. But it means to have it, in the long run.

GERALD: You mean by increasing demands for higher wages?

JOB ARTHUR: Yes, perhaps that's one road.

GERALD: Do you see any other?

JOB ARTHUR: Not just for the present.

GERALD: But later on?

JOB ARTHUR: I can't say about that. The men will be quiet enough for a bit, if it's alright about the office men, you know.

GERALD: Probably. But have Barlow and Walsall's men any special grievance apart from the rest of the miners?

JOB ARTHUR: I don't know. They've no liking for you, you know, sir.

GERALD: Why?

JOB ARTHUR: They think you've got a down on them.

GERALD: Why should they?

JOB ARTHUR: I don't know, sir; but they do.

GERALD: So they have a personal feeling against me? You don't think all the colliers are the same, all over the country?

JOB ARTHUR: I think there's a good deal of feeling

GERALD: Of wanting their own back?

JOB ARTHUR: That's it.

GERALD: But what can they do? I don't see what they can do. They can go out on strike, but they've done that before, and the owners, at a pinch, can stand it better than they can. As for the ruin of the industry, if they do ruin it, it falls heaviest on them. In fact, it leaves them destitute. There's nothing they can do, you know, that doesn't hit them worse than it hits us.

JOB ARTHUR: I know there's something in that. But if they had a strong man to head them, you see

GERALD: Yes, I've heard a lot about that strong man, but I've never come across any signs of him, you know. I don't believe in one strong man appearing out of so many little men. All men are pretty big in an age, or in a movement, which produces a really big man. And Labour is a great swarm of hopelessly little men. That's how I see it.

JOB ARTHUR: I'm not so sure about that.

GERALD: I am. Labour is a thing that can't have a head. It's a sort of unwieldy monster that's bound to run its skull against the wall sooner or later, and knock out what bit of brain it's got. You see, you need wit and courage and real understanding if you're going to do anything positive. And Labour has none of these things, certainly it shows no sign of them.

JOB ARTHUR: Yes, when it has a chance, I think you'll see plenty of courage and plenty of understanding.

GERALD: It always has a chance. And where one sees a bit of courage, there's no understanding; and where there's some understanding, there's absolutely no courage. It's hopeless, you know, it would be far best if they'd all give it up, and try a new line.

JOB ARTHUR: I don't think they will.

GERALD: No, I don't either. They'll make a mess, and when they've made it, they'll never get out of it. They can't, they're too stupid.

JOB ARTHUR: They've never had a try yet.

GERALD: They're trying every day. They just simply couldn't control modern industry, they haven't the intelligence. They've no life intelligence. The owners may have little enough, but Labour has none. They're just mechanical little things that can make one or two motions, and they're done. They've no more idea of life than a lawn-mower has.

JOB ARTHUR: It remains to be seen.

GERALD: No, it doesn't. It's perfectly obvious, there's nothing remains to be seen. All that Labour is capable of, is smashing things up. And even for that I don't believe it has either energy or the courage or the bit of necessary passion, or slap-dash, call it whatever you will. However, we'll see.

JOB ARTHUR: Yes, sir. Perhaps you see now why you're not so very popular, Mr Gerald.

GERALD: We can't all be popular, Job Arthur. You're very high up in popularity, I believe.

JOB ARTHUR: Not so very. They listen to me a bit. But you never know when they'll let you down. I know they'll let me down one day, so it won't be a surprise.

GERALD: I should think not.

JOB ARTHUR: But about the office men, Mr Gerald. You think it'll be alright?

GERALD: Oh, yes, that'll be alright.

JOB ARTHUR: Easiest for this time, anyhow, sir. We don't want bloodshed, do we?

GERALD: I shouldn't mind at all. It might clear the way to something. But I have absolutely no belief in the power of Labour even to bring about anything so positive as bloodshed.

JOB ARTHUR: I don't know about that, I don't know. Well.

GERALD: Have another drink before you go. Yes, do. Help yourself.

JOB ARTHUR: Well, if you're so pressing. (Helps himself.) Here's luck, all!

ALL: Thanks.

GERALD: Take a cigar, there's the box. Go on, take a handful, fill your case.

JOB ARTHUR: They're a great luxury nowadays, aren't they? Almost beyond a man like me.

GERALD: Yes, that's the worst of not being a bloated capitalist. Never mind, you'll be a Cabinet Minister some day. Oh, alright, I'll open the door for you.

JOB ARTHUR: Oh, don't trouble. Good night, good night.

Exeunt JOB ARTHUR and GERALD.

OLIVER: Oh God, what a world to live in!

ANABEL: I rather liked him. What is he?

OLIVER: Checkweighman, local secretary for the Miners' Federation, plays the violin well, although he was a collier, and it spoilt his hands. They're a musical family.

ANABEL: But isn't he rather nice?

OLIVER: I don't like him. But I confess he's a study. He's the modern Judas.

ANABEL: Don't you think he likes Gerald?

OLIVER: I'm sure he does. The way he suns himself here, like a cat purring in his luxuriation.

ANABEL: Yes, I don't mind it. It shows a certain sensitiveness and a certain taste.

OLIVER: Yes, he has both, touch of the artist, as Mrs Barlow says. He loves refinement, culture, breeding, all those things, loves them, and a presence, a fine free manner.

ANABEL: But that is nice in him.

OLIVER: Quite. But what he loves, and what he admires, and what he aspires to, he must betray. It's his fatality. He lives for the moment when he can kiss Gerald in the Garden of Olives, or wherever it was.

ANABEL: But Gerald shouldn't be kissed.

OLIVER: That's what I say.

ANABEL: And that's what his mother means as well, I suppose.

Enter GERALD.

GERALD: Well, you've heard the voice of the people.

ANABEL: He isn't the people.

GERALD: I think he is, myself, the epitome.

OLIVER: No, he's a special type.

GERALD: Ineffectual, don't you think?

ANABEL: How pleased you are, Gerald! How pleased you are with yourself! You love the turn with him.

GERALD: It's rather stimulating, you know.

ANABEL: It oughtn't to be, then.

OLIVER: He's your Judas, and you love him.

GERALD: Nothing so deep. He's just a sort of Æolian harp that sings to the temper of the wind. I find him amusing.

ANABEL: I think it's boring.

OLIVER: And I think it's nasty.

GERALD: I believe you're both jealous of him. What do you think of the British working man, Oliver?

OLIVER: It seems to me he's in nearly as bad a way as the British employer: he's nearly as much beside the point.

GERALD: What point?

OLIVER: Oh, just life.

GERALD: That's too vague, my boy. Do you think they'll ever make a bust-up?

OLIVER: I can't tell. I don't see any good in it, if they do.

GERALD: It might clear the way, and it might block the way for ever: depends what comes through. But, sincerely, I don't think they've got it in them.

ANABEL: They may have something better.

GERALD: That suggestion doesn't interest me, Anabel. Ah well, we shall see what we shall see. Have a whisky and soda with me, Oliver, and let the troubled course of this evening run to a smooth close. It's quite like old times. Aren't you smoking, Anabel?

ANABEL: No, thanks.

GERALD: I believe you're a reformed character. So it won't be like old times, after all.

ANABEL: I don't want old times. I want new ones.

GERALD: Wait till Job Arthur has risen like Antichrist, and proclaimed the resurrection of the gods. Do you see Job Arthur proclaiming Dionysus and Aphrodite?

ANABEL: It bores me. I don't like your mood. Good night.

GERALD: Oh, don't go.

ANABEL: Yes, good night.

Exit ANABEL.

OLIVER: She's not reformed, Gerald. She's the same old moral character, moral to the last bit of her, really, as she always was.

GERALD: Is that what it is? But one must be moral.

OLIVER: Oh, yes. Oliver Cromwell wasn't as moral as Anabel is, nor such an iconoclast.

GERALD: Poor old Anabel!

OLIVER: How she hates the dark gods!

GERALD: And yet they cast a spell over her. Poor old Anabel! Well, Oliver, is Bacchus the father of whisky?

OLIVER: I don't know. I don't like you either. You seem to smile all over yourself. It's objectionable. Good night.

GERALD: Oh, look here, this is censorious.

OLIVER: You smile to yourself.

Exit OLIVER.

CURTAIN

ACT III

SCENE I

An old park. Early evening. In the background a low Georgian hall, which has been turned into offices for the Company, shows windows already lighted. GERALD and ANABEL walk along the path.

ANABEL: How beautiful this old park is!

GERALD: Yes, it is beautiful, seems so far away from everywhere, if one doesn't remember that the hall is turned into offices. No one has lived here since I was a little boy. I remember going to a Christmas party at the Walsalls'.

ANABEL: Has it been shut up so long?

GERALD: The Walsalls didn't like it, too near the ugliness. They were county, you know, we never were: Father never gave Mother a chance, there. And besides, the place is damp, cellars full of water.

ANABEL: Even now?

GERALD: No, not now, they've been drained. But the place would be too damp for a dwelling-house. It's alright as offices. They burn enormous fires. The rooms are quite charming. This is what happens to the stately homes of England, they buzz with inky clerks, or their equivalent. Stateliness is on its last legs.

ANABEL: Yes, it grieves me, though I should be bored if I had to be stately, I think. Isn't it beautiful in this light, like an eighteenth-century aquatint? I'm sure no age was as ugly as this, since the world began.

GERALD: For pure ugliness, certainly not. And I believe none has been so filthy to live in. Let us sit down a minute, shall we? and watch the rooks fly home. It always stirs sad, sentimental feelings in me.

ANABEL: So it does in me. Listen! one can hear the coal-carts on the road, and the brook, and the dull noise of the town, and the beating of New London pit, and voices, and the rooks, and yet it is so still. We seem so still here, don't we?

GERALD: Yes.

ANABEL: Don't you think we've been wrong?

GERALD: How?

ANABEL: In the way we've lived, and the way we've loved.

GERALD: It hasn't been heaven, has it? Yet, I don't know that we've been wrong, Anabel. We had it to go through.

ANABEL: Perhaps. And, yes, we've been wrong too.

GERALD: Probably. Only, I don't feel it like that.

ANABEL: Then I think you ought. You ought to feel you've been wrong.

GERALD: Yes, probably. Only, I don't. I can't help it. I think we've gone the way we had to go, following our own natures.

ANABEL: And where has it landed us?

GERALD: Here.

ANABEL: And where is that?

GERALD: Just on this bench in the park, looking at the evening.

ANABEL: But what next?

GERALD: God knows! Why trouble?

ANABEL: One must trouble. I want to feel sure.

GERALD: What of?

ANABEL: Of you and of myself.

GERALD: Then be sure.

ANABEL: But I can't. Think of the past, what it's been.

GERALD: This isn't the past.

ANABEL: But what is it? Is there anything sure in it? Is there any real happiness?

GERALD: Why not?

ANABEL: But how can you ask? Think of what our life has been.

GERALD: I don't want to.

ANABEL: No, you don't. But what do you want?

GERALD: I'm alright, you know, sitting here like this.

ANABEL: But one can't sit here for ever, can one?

GERALD: I don't want to.

ANABEL: And what will you do when we leave here?

GERALD: God knows! Don't worry me. Be still a bit.

ANABEL: But I'm worried. You don't love me.

GERALD: I won't argue it.

ANABEL: And I'm not happy.

GERALD: Why not, Anabel?

ANABEL: Because you don't love me, and I can't forget.

GERALD: I do love you, and to-night I've forgotten.

ANABEL: Then make me forget, too. Make me happy.

GERALD: I can't make you and you know it.

ANABEL: Yes, you can. It's your business to make me happy. I've made you happy.

GERALD: You want to make me unhappy.

ANABEL: I do think you're the last word in selfishness. If I say I can't forget, you merely say, "I've forgotten"; and if I say I'm unhappy, all you can answer is that I want to make you unhappy. I don't in the least. I want to be happy myself. But you don't help me.

GERALD: There is no help for it, you see. If you were happy with me here you'd be happy. As you aren't, nothing will make you, not genuinely.

ANABEL: And that's all you care.

GERALD: No, I wish we could both be happy at the same moment. But apparently we can't.

ANABEL: And why not? Because you're selfish, and think of nothing but yourself and your own feelings.

GERALD: If it is so, it is so.

ANABEL: Then we shall never be happy.

GERALD: Then we shan't. (A pause.)

ANABEL: Then what are we going to do?

GERALD: Do?

ANABEL: Do you want me to be with you?

GERALD: Yes.

ANABEL: Are you sure?

GERALD: Yes.

ANABEL: Then why don't you want me to be happy?

GERALD: If you'd only be happy, here and now

ANABEL: How can I?

GERALD: How can't you? You've got a devil inside you.

ANABEL: Then make me not have a devil.

GERALD: I've known you long enough, and known myself long enough, to know I can make you nothing at all, Anabel: neither can you make me. If the happiness isn't there, well, we shall have to wait for it, like a dispensation. It probably means we shall have to hate each other a little more. I suppose hate is a real process.

ANABEL: Yes, I know you believe more in hate than in love.

GERALD: Nobody is more weary of hate than I am, and yet we can't fix our own hour, when we shall leave off hating and fighting. It has to work itself out in us.

ANABEL: But I don't want to hate and fight with you any more. I don't believe in it, not any more.

GERALD: It's a cleansing process, like Aristotle's Katharsis. We shall hate ourselves clean at last, I suppose.

ANABEL: Why aren't you clean now? Why can't you love? (He laughs.) Do you love me?

GERALD: Yes.

ANABEL: Do you want to be with me for ever?

GERALD: Yes.

ANABEL: Sure?

GERALD: Quite sure.

ANABEL: Why are you so cool about it?

GERALD: I'm not. I'm only sure, which you are not.

ANABEL: Yes, I am, I want to be married to you.

GERALD: I know you want me to want you to be married to me. But whether off your own bat you have a positive desire that way, I'm not sure. You keep something back, some sort of female reservation, like a dagger up your sleeve. You want to see me in transports of love for you.

ANABEL: How can you say so? There, you see, there, this is the man that pretends to love me, and then says I keep a dagger up my sleeve. You liar!

GERALD: I do love you, and you do keep a dagger up your sleeve, some devilish little female reservation which spies at me from a distance, in your soul, all the time, as if I were an enemy.

ANABEL: How can you say so? Doesn't it show what you must be yourself? Doesn't it show? What is there in your soul?

GERALD: I don't know.

ANABEL: Love, pure love? Do you pretend it's love?

GERALD: I'm so tired of this.

ANABEL: So am I, dead tired: you self-deceiving, self-complacent thing. Ha! aren't you just the same. You haven't altered one scrap, not a scrap.

GERALD: Alright, you are always free to change yourself.

ANABEL: I have changed, I am better, I do love you, I love you wholly and unselfishly, I do, and I want a good new life with you.

GERALD: You're terribly wrapped up in your new goodness. I wish you'd make up your mind to be downright bad.

ANABEL: Ha! Do you? You'd soon see. You'd soon see where you'd be if. There's somebody coming. (Rises.)

GERALD: Never mind; it's the clerks leaving work, I suppose. Sit still.

ANABEL: Won't you go?

GERALD: No. (A man draws near, followed by another.) Good evening.

CLERK: Good evening, sir. (Passes on.) Good evening, Mr Barlow.

ANABEL: They are afraid.

GERALD: I suppose their consciences are uneasy about this strike.

ANABEL: Did you come to sit here just to catch them, like a spider waiting for them?

GERALD: No. I wanted to speak to Breffitt.

ANABEL: I believe you're capable of any horridness.

GERALD: Alright, you believe it. (Two more figures approach.) Good evening.

CLERKS: Good night, sir. (One passes, one stops.) Good evening, Mr Barlow. Er, did you want to see Mr Breffitt, sir?

GERALD: Not particularly.

CLERK: Oh! He'll be out directly, sir, if you'd like me to go back and tell him you wanted him.

GERALD: No, thank you.

CLERK: Good night, sir. Excuse me asking.

GERALD: Good night.

ANABEL: Who is Mr Breffitt?

GERALD: He is the chief clerk, and cashier, one of Father's old pillars of society.

ANABEL: Don't you like him?

GERALD: Not much.

ANABEL: Why? You seem to dislike very easily.

GERALD: Oh, they all used to try to snub me, these old buffers. They detest me like poison, because I am different from Father.

ANABEL: I believe you enjoy being detested.

GERALD: I do. (Another clerk approaches, hesitates, stops.)

CLERK: Good evening, sir. Good evening, Mr Barlow. Er, did you want anybody at the office, sir? We're just closing.

GERALD: No, I didn't want anybody.

CLERK: Oh, no, sir. I see. Er, by the way, sir, er, I hope you don't think this, er, bother about an increase, this strike threat, started in the office.

GERALD: Where did it start?

CLERK: I should think it started, where it usually starts, Mr Barlow, among a few loud-mouthed people who think they can do as they like with the men. They're only using the office men as a cry, that's all. They've no interest in us. They want to show their power. That's how it is, sir.

GERALD: Oh, yes.

CLERK: We're powerless, if they like to make a cry out of us.

GERALD: Quite.

CLERK: We're as much put out about it as anybody.

GERALD: Of course.

CLERK: Yes, well, good night, sir. (Clerks draw near, there is a sound of loud young voices and bicycle bells. Bicycles sweep past.)

CLERKS: Good night, sir. Good night, sir.

GERALD: Good night. They're very bucked to see me sitting here with a woman, a young lady as they'll say. I guess your name will be flying round to-morrow. They stop partly to have a good look at you. Do they know you, do you think?

ANABEL: Sure.

CLERKS: Mr Breffitt's just coming, sir. Good night, sir. Good night, sir. (Another bicycle passes.)

ANABEL: The bicycles don't see us. Isn't it rather hateful to be a master? The attitude of them all is so ugly. I can quite see that it makes you rather a bully.

GERALD: I suppose it does. (Figure of a large man approaches.)

BREFFITT: Oh, ah, it's Mr Gerald! I couldn't make out who it was. Were you coming up to the office, sir? Do you want me to go back with you?

GERALD: No, thank you, I just wanted a word with you about this agitation. It'll do just as well here. It's a pity it started, that the office should have set it going, Breffitt.

BREFFITT: It's none of the office's doing, I think you'll find, Mr Gerald. The office men did nothing but ask for a just advance, at any rate, times and prices being what they are, I consider it a fair advance. If the men took it up, it's because they've got a set of loud-mouthed blatherers and agitators among them like Job Arthur Freer, who deserve to be hung, and hanging they'd get, if I could have the judging of them.

GERALD: Well, it's very unfortunate, because we can't give the clerks their increase now, you know.

BREFFITT: Can't you? can't you? I can't see that it would be anything out of the way, if I say what I think.

GERALD: No. They won't get any increase now. It shouldn't have been allowed to become a public cry with the colliers. We can't give in now.

BREFFITT: Have the Board decided that?

GERALD: They have, on my advice.

BREFFITT: Hm! then the men will come out.

GERALD: We will see.

BREFFITT: It's trouble for nothing, it's trouble that could be avoided. The clerks could have their advance, and it would hurt nobody.

GERALD: Too late now. I suppose if the men come out, the clerks will come out with them?

BREFFITT: They'll have to, they'll have to.

GERALD: If they do, we may then make certain alterations in the office staff which have needed making for some time.

BREFFITT: Very good, very good. I know what you mean. I don't know how your father bears all this, Mr Gerald.

GERALD: We keep it from him as much as possible. You'll let the clerks know the decision. And if they stay out with the men, I'll go over the list of the staff with you. It has needed revising for a long time.

BREFFITT: I know what you mean, I know what you mean, I believe I understand the firm's interest in my department. I ought, after forty years studying it. I've studied the firm's interests for forty years, Mr Gerald. I'm not likely to forget them now.

GERALD: Of course.

BREFFITT: But I think it's a mistake, I think it's a mistake, and I'm bound to say it, to let a great deal of trouble rise for a very small cause. The clerks might have had what they reasonably asked for.

GERALD: Well, it's too late now.

BREFFITT: I suppose it is, I suppose it is. I hope you'll remember, sir, that I've put the interest of the firm before everything, before every consideration.

GERALD: Of course, Breffitt.

BREFFITT: But you've not had any liking for the office staff, I'm afraid, sir, not since your father put you amongst us for a few months. Well, sir, we shall weather this gale, I hope, as we've weathered those in the past. Times don't become better, do they? Men are an ungrateful lot, and these agitators should be lynched. They would, if I had my way.

GERALD: Yes, of course. Don't wait.

BREFFITT: Good night to you.

Exit BREFFITT.

GERALD: Good night.

ANABEL: He's the last, apparently.

GERALD: We'll hope so.

ANABEL: He puts you in a fury.

GERALD: It's his manner. My father spoilt them, abominable old limpets. And they're so self-righteous. They think I'm a sort of criminal who has instigated this new devilish system which runs everything so close and cuts it so fine, as if they hadn't made this inevitable by their shameless carelessness and wastefulness in the past. He may well boast of his forty years, forty years' crass, stupid wastefulness.

Two or three more clerks pass, talking till they approach the seat, then becoming silent after bidding good night.

ANABEL: But aren't you a bit sorry for them?

GERALD: Why? If they're poor, what does it matter in a world of chaos?

ANABEL: And aren't you an obstinate ass not to give them the bit they want. It's mere stupid obstinacy.

GERALD: It may be. I call it policy.

ANABEL: Men always do call their obstinacy policy.

GERALD: Well, I don't care what happens. I wish things would come to a head. I only fear they won't.

ANABEL: Aren't you rather wicked? Asking for strife?

GERALD: I hope I am. It's quite a relief to me to feel that I may be wicked. I fear I'm not. I can see them all anticipating victory, in their low-down fashion wanting to crow their low-down crowings. I'm afraid I feel it's a righteous cause, to cut a lot of little combs before I die.

ANABEL: But if they're in the right in what they want?

GERALD: In the right, in the right! They're just greedy, incompetent, stupid, gloating in a sense of the worst sort of power. They're like vicious children, who would like to kill their parents so that they could have the run of the larder. The rest is just cant.

ANABEL: If you're the parent in the case, I must say you flow over with loving-kindness for them.

GERALD: I don't, I detest them. I only hope they will fight. If they would, I'd have some respect for them. But you'll see what it will be.

ANABEL: I wish I needn't, for it's very sickening.

GERALD: Sickening beyond expression.

ANABEL: I wish we could go right away.

GERALD: So do I, if one could get oneself out of this. But one can't. It's the same wherever you have industrialism, and you have industrialism everywhere, whether it's Timbuctoo or Paraguay or Antananarivo.

ANABEL: No, it isn't: you exaggerate.

JOB ARTHUR (suddenly approaching from the other side): Good evening, Mr Barlow. I heard you were in here. Could I have a word with you?

GERALD: Get on with it, then.

JOB ARTHUR: Is it right that you won't meet the clerks?

GERALD: Yes.

JOB ARTHUR: Not in any way?

GERALD: Not in any way whatsoever.

JOB ARTHUR: But, I thought I understood from you the other night

GERALD: It's all the same what you understood.

JOB ARTHUR: Then you take it back, sir?

GERALD: I take nothing back, because I gave nothing.

JOB ARTHUR: Oh, excuse me, excuse me, sir. You said it would be alright about the clerks. This lady heard you say it.

GERALD: Don't you call witnesses against me. Besides, what does it matter to you? What in the name of

JOB ARTHUR: Well, sir, you said it would be alright, and I went on that

GERALD: You went on that! Where did you go to?

JOB ARTHUR: The men'll be out on Monday.

GERALD: So shall I.

JOB ARTHUR: Oh, yes, but, where's it going to end?

GERALD: Do you want me to prophesy? When did I set up for a public prophet?

JOB ARTHUR: I don't know, sir. But perhaps you're doing more than you know. There's a funny feeling just now among the men.

GERALD: So I've heard before. Why should I concern myself with their feelings? Am I to cry when every collier bumps his funny-bone, or to laugh?

JOB ARTHUR: It's no laughing matter, you see.

GERALD: And I'm sure it's no crying matter, unless you want to cry, do you see?

JOB ARTHUR: Ah, but, very likely, it wouldn't be me who would cry. You don't know what might happen, now.

GERALD: I'm waiting for something to happen. I should like something to happen, very much, very much indeed.

JOB ARTHUR: Yes, but perhaps you'd be sorry if it did happen.

GERALD: Is that a warning or a threat?

JOB ARTHUR: I don't know, it might be a bit of both. What I mean to say

GERALD (suddenly seizing him by the scruff of the neck and shaking him): What do you mean to say? I mean you to say less, do you see? a great deal less, do you see? You've run on with your saying long enough: that clock had better run down. So stop your sayings, stop your sayings, I tell you, or you'll have them shaken out of you, shaken out of you, shaken out of you, do you see? (Suddenly flings him aside.)

JOB ARTHUR, staggering, falls.

ANABEL: Oh no! oh, no!

GERALD: Now get up, Job Arthur; and get up wiser than you went down. You've played your little game and your little tricks and made your little sayings long enough. You're going to stop now. We've had quite enough of strong men of your stamp, Job Arthur, quite enough, such Labour leaders as you.

JOB ARTHUR: You'll be sorry, Mr Barlow, you'll be sorry. You'll wish you'd not attacked me.

GERALD: Don't you trouble about me and my sorrow. Mind your own.

JOB ARTHUR: You will, you'll be sorry. You'll be sorry for what you've done. You'll wish you'd never begun this.

GERALD: Begun, begun? I'd like to finish, too, that I would. I'd like to finish with you, too, I warn you.

JOB ARTHUR: I warn you, I warn you. You won't go on much longer. Every parish has its own vermin.

GERALD: Vermin?

JOB ARTHUR: Every parish has its own vermin; it lies with every parish to destroy its own. We shan't have a clean parish till we've destroyed the vermin we've got.

GERALD: Vermin? The fool's raving. Vermin! Another phrase-maker, by God! Another phrase-maker to lead the people. Vermin? What vermin? I know quite well what I mean by vermin, Job Arthur. But what do you mean? Vermin? Explain yourself.

JOB ARTHUR: Yes, vermin. Vermin is what lives on other people's lives, living on their lives and profiting by it. We've got 'em in every parish, vermin, I say, that live on the sweat and blood of the people, live on it, and get rich on it, get rich through living on other people's lives, the lives of the working men, living on the bodies of the working men, that's vermin, if it isn't, what is it? And every parish must destroy its own, every parish must destroy its own vermin.

GERALD: The phrase, my God! the phrase.

JOB ARTHUR: Phrase or no phrase, there it is, and face it out if you can. There it is, there's not one in every parish, there's more than one, there's a number

GERALD (suddenly kicking him): Go! (Kicks him.) Go! (Kicks him.) Go! (JOB ARTHUR falls.) Get out! (Kicks him.)Get out, I say! Get out, I tell you! Get out! Get out! Vermin! Vermin! I'll vermin you! I'll put my foot through your phrases. Get up, I say, get up and go, go!

JOB ARTHUR: It'll be you as'll go, this time.

GERALD: What? What? By God! I'll kick you out of this park like a rotten bundle if you don't get up and go.

ANABEL: No, Gerald, no. Don't forget yourself. It's enough now. It's enough now. Come away. Do come away. Come away, leave him

JOB ARTHUR (still on the ground): It's your turn to go. It's you as'll go, this time.

GERALD (looking at him): One can't even tread on you.

ANABEL: Don't, Gerald, don't, don't look at him. Don't say any more, you, Job Arthur. Come away, Gerald. Come away, come, do come.

GERALD (turning): That a human being! My God! But he's right, it's I who go. It's we who go, Anabel. He's still there. My God! a human being!

CURTAIN

SCENE II

Market-place as in Act I. WILLIE HOUGHTON, addressing a large crowd of men from the foot of the obelisk.

WILLIE: And now you're out on strike, now you've been out for a week pretty nearly, what further are you? I heard a great deal of talk about what you were going to do. Well, what are you going to do? You don't know. You've not the smallest idea. You haven't any idea whatsoever. You've got your leaders. Now then, Job Arthur, throw a little light on the way in front, will you: for it seems to me we're lost in a bog. Which way are we to steer? Come, give the word, and let's gee-up.

JOB ARTHUR: You ask me which way we are to go. I say we can't go our own way, because of the obstacles that lie in front. You've got to remove the obstacles from the way.

WILLIE: So said Balaam's ass. But you're not an ass, beg pardon, and you're not Balaam, you're Job. And we've all got to be little Jobs, learning how to spell patience backwards. We've lost our jobs and we've found a Job. It's picking up a scorpion when you're looking for an egg. Tell us what you propose doing. . . . Remove an obstacle from the way! What obstacle? And whose way?

JOB ARTHUR: I think it's pretty plain what the obstacle is.

WILLIE: Oh ay. Tell us then.

JOB ARTHUR: The obstacle to Labour is Capital.

WILLIE: And how are we going to put salt on Capital's tail?

JOB ARTHUR: By Labour we mean us working men; and by Capital we mean those that derive benefit from us, take the cream off us and leave us the skim.

WILLIE: Oh yes.

JOB ARTHUR: So that, if you're going to remove the obstacle, you've got to remove the masters, and all that belongs to them. Does everybody agree with me?

VOICES (loud): Ah, we do, yes, we do that, we do an' a', yi, yi, that's it!

WILLIE: Agreed unanimously. But how are we going to do it? Do you propose to send for Williamson's furniture van, to pack them in? I should think one pantechnicon would do, just for this parish. I'll drive. Who'll be the vanmen to lift and carry?

JOB ARTHUR: It's no use fooling. You've fooled for thirty years, and we're no further. What's got to be done will have to be begun. It's for every man to sweep in front of his own doorstep. You can't call your neighbours dirty till you've washed your own face. Every parish has got its own vermin, and it's the business of every parish to get rid of its own.

VOICES: That's it, that's it, that's the ticket, that's the style!

WILLIE: And are you going to comb 'em out, or do you propose to use Keating's?

VOICES: Shut it! Shut it up! Stop thy face! Hold thy gab! Go on, Job Arthur.

JOB ARTHUR: How it's got to be done is for us all to decide. I'm not one for violence, except it's a force-put. But it's like this. We've been travelling for years to where we stand now, and here the road stops. There's only room for one at a time on this path. There's a precipice below and a rock-face above. And in front of us stand the masters. Now there's three things we can do. We can either throw ourselves over the precipice; or we can lie down and let the masters walk over us; or we can get on.

WILLIE: Yes. That's alright. But how are you going to get on?

JOB ARTHUR: Well, we've either got to throw the obstacle down the cliff, or walk over it.

VOICES: Ay, ay, ay, yes, that's a fact.

WILLIE: I quite follow you, Job Arthur. You've either got to do for the masters, or else just remove them, and put them somewhere else.

VOICES: Ged rid on 'em, drop 'em down the shaft, sink 'em, ha' done wi' 'em, drop 'em down the shaft, bust the beggars, what do you do wi' vermin?

WILLIE: Supposing you begin. Supposing you take Gerald Barlow, and hang him up from this lamp-post, with a piece of coal in his mouth for a sacrament

VOICES: Ay, serve him right, serve the beggar right! Shove it down 's throttle, ay!

WILLIE: Supposing you do it, supposing you've done it, and supposing you aren't caught and punished, even supposing that, what are you going to do next? that's the point.

JOB ARTHUR: We know what we're going to do. Once we can get our hands free, we know what we're going to do.

WILLIE: Yes, so do I. You're either going to make such a mess that we shall never get out of it, which I don't think you will do, for the English working man is the soul of obedience and order, and he'd behave himself to-morrow as if he was at Sunday school, no matter what he does to-day. No, what you'll do, Job Arthur, you'll set up another lot of masters, such a jolly sight worse than what we've got now. I'd rather be mastered by Gerald Barlow, if it comes to mastering, than by Job Arthur Freer, oh, such a lot! You'll be far less free with Job Arthur for your boss than ever you were with Gerald Barlow. You'll be far more degraded. In fact, though I've preached socialism in the market-place for thirty years, if you're going to start killing the masters to set yourselves up for bosses, why, kill me along with the masters. For I'd rather die with somebody who has one tiny little spark of decency left, though it is a little tiny spark, than live to triumph with those that have none.

VOICES: Shut thy face, Houghton, shut it up, shut him up, hustle the beggar! Hoi! hoi-ee! whoo! whoam-it, whoam-it! whoo! bow-wow! wet-whiskers!

WILLIE: And it's no use you making fools of yourselves (His words are heard through an ugly, jeering, cold commotion.)

VOICE (loudly): He's comin'.

VOICES: Who?

VOICE: Barlow. See 's motor? comin' up, sithee?

WILLIE: If you've any sense left (Suddenly and violently disappears.)

VOICES: Sorry! he's comin', 's comin', sorry, ah! Who's in? That's Turton drivin', yi, he's behind wi' a woman, ah, he's comin', he'll non go back, hold on. Sorry! wheer's 'e comin'? up from Loddo, ay, (The cries die down, the motor car slowly comes into sight, OLIVER driving, GERALD and ANABEL behind. The men stand in a mass in the way.)

OLIVER: Mind yourself, there. (Laughter.)

GERALD: Go ahead, Oliver.

VOICE: What's yer 'urry?

Crowd sways and surges on the car. OLIVER is suddenly dragged out. GERALD stands up, he, too, is seized from behind, he wrestles, is torn out of his great-coat, then falls, disappears. Loud cries, "Hi! hoi! hoi-ee!" all the while. The car shakes and presses uneasily.

VOICE: Stop the blazin' motor, somebody.

VOICE: Here y'are! hold a minute. (A man jumps in and stops the engine, he drops in the driver's seat.)

COLLIER (outside the car): Step down, miss.

ANABEL: I am Mrs Barlow.

COLLIER: Missis, then. (Laugh.) Step down, lead 'er forrard. Take 'em forrard, take 'em forrard.

JOB ARTHUR: Ay, make a road.

GERALD: You're makin' a proper fool of yourself now, Freer.

JOB ARTHUR: You've brought it on yourself. You've made fools of plenty of men.

COLLIERS: Come on, now, come on! Whoa! whoa! he's a jibber, go pretty now, go pretty!

VOICES (suddenly): Lay hold o' Houghton, nab 'im, seize 'im, rats! rats! bring 'im forrard!

ANABEL (in a loud, clear voice): I never knew anything so ridiculous.

VOICES (falsetto): Ridiculous! Oh, ridiculous! Mind the step, dear! I'm Mrs Barlow! Oh, are you? Tweet, tweet!

JOB ARTHUR: Make a space, boys, make a space. (He stands with prisoners in a cleared space before the obelisk.) Now, now, quiet a minute, we want to ask a few questions of these gentlemen.

VOICES: Quiet! quiet, Sh-h-h! Sh-h-h! Answer pretty, answer pretty now! Quiet! Shh-h-h!

JOB ARTHUR: We want to ask you, Mr Gerald Barlow, why you have given occasion for this present trouble?

GERALD: You are a fool.

VOICES: Oh! oh! naughty Barlow! naughty baa-lamb, answer pretty, answer pretty, be good baa-lamb, baa, baa! answer pretty when gentleman asks you.

JOB ARTHUR: Quiet a bit. Sh-h-h! We put this plain question to you, Mr Barlow. Why did you refuse to give the clerks this just and fair advance, when you knew that by refusing you would throw three thousand men out of employment?

GERALD: You are a fool, I say.

VOICES: Oh! oh! won't do, won't do, Barlow, wrong answer, wrong answer, be good baa-lamb, naughty boy, naughty boy!

JOB ARTHUR: Quiet a bit, now! If three thousand men ask you a just, straightforward question, do you consider they've no right to an answer?

GERALD: I would answer you with my foot.

VOICES (amid a threatening scuffle): Da-di-da! Hark ye, hark ye! Oh, whoa, whoa a bit! won't do! won't do! naughty, naughty, say you're sorry, say you're sorry, kneel and say you're sorry, kneel and beg pardon!

JOB ARTHUR: Hold on a bit, keep clear!

VOICES: Make him kneel, make him kneel, on his knees with him!

JOB ARTHUR: I think you'd better kneel down.

The crowd press on GERALD, he struggles, they hit him behind the knees, force him down.

OLIVER: This is shameful and unnecessary.

VOICES: All of 'em, on your knees, all of 'em, on their knees!

They seize OLIVER and WILLIE and ANABEL, hustling. ANABEL kneels quietly, the others struggle.

WILLIE: Well, of all the damned, dirty, cowardly

VOICES: Shut up, Houghton, shut him up, squeeze him!

OLIVER: Get off me, let me alone, I'll kneel.

VOICES: Good little doggies, nice doggies, kneel and beg pardon, yap-yap, answer, make him answer!

JOB ARTHUR (holding up his hand for silence): It would be better if you answered straight off, Barlow. We want to know why you prevented that advance?

VOICES (after a pause): Nip his neck! Make him yelp!

OLIVER: Let me answer, then. Because it's worse, perhaps, to be bullied by three thousand men than by one man.

VOICES: Oh! oh! dog keeps barking, stuff his mouth, stop him up, here's a bit of paper, answer. Barlow, nip his neck, stuff his mug, make him yelp, cork the bottle!

They press a lump of newspaper into OLIVER'S mouth, and bear down on GERALD.

JOB ARTHUR: Quiet, quiet, quiet, a minute, everybody. We give him a minute, we give him a minute to answer.

VOICES: Give him a minute, a holy minute, say your prayers, Barlow, you've got a minute, tick-tick, says the clock, time him!

JOB ARTHUR: Keep quiet.

WILLIE: Of all the damned, cowardly

VOICES: Sh-h-h! Squeeze him, throttle him! Silence is golden, Houghton. Close the shutters, Willie's dead. Dry up, wet-whiskers!

JOB ARTHUR: You've fifteen seconds.

VOICES: There's a long, long trail a-winding

JOB ARTHUR: The minute's up. We ask you again, Gerald Barlow, why you refused a just and fair demand, when you know it was against the wishes of three thousand men all as good as yourself?

VOICES: And a sight better, I don't think, we're not all vermin, we're not all crawlers, living off the sweat of other folks, we're not all parish vermin, parish vermin.

JOB ARTHUR: And on what grounds you think you have no occasion to answer the straightforward question we put you here?

ANABEL (after a pause): Answer them, Gerald. What's the use of prolonging this?

GERALD: I've nothing to answer.

VOICES: Nothing to answer, Gerald, darling, Gerald, duckie, oh, lovey-dovey, I've nothing to answer, no, by God, no, by God, he hasna, nowt to answer, ma'e him find summat, then, answer for him, gi'e him 's answer, let him ha'e it, go on, mum, mum, lovey-dovey, rub his nose in it, kiss the dirt, ducky, bend him down, rub his nose in, he's saying something, oh no, he isn't, sorry I spoke, bend him down!

JOB ARTHUR: Quiet a bit, quiet, everybody, he's got to answer, keep quiet. Now (A silence.) Now then, Barlow, will you answer, or won't you? (Silence.)

ANABEL: Answer them, Gerald, never mind.

VOICES: Sh-h-h! Sh-h-h! (Silence.)

JOB ARTHUR: You won't answer, Barlow?

VOICE: Down the beggar!

VOICES: Down him, put his nose down, flatten him!

The crowd surges and begins to howl, they sway dangerously, GERALD is spread-eagled on the ground, face down.

JOB ARTHUR: Back, back, back a minute, back, back! (They recoil.)

WILLIE: I hope there's a God in heaven.

VOICES: Put him down, flatten him!

WILLIE is flattened on the ground.

JOB ARTHUR: Now then, now then, if you won't answer, Barlow, I can't stand here for you any more. Take your feet off him, boys, and turn him over. Turn him over, let us look at him. Let us see if he can speak. (They turn him over, with another scuffle.) Now then, Barlow, you can see the sky above you. Now do you think you're going to play with three thousand men, with their lives and with their souls? now do you think you're going to answer them with your foot? do you, do you?

The crowd has begun to sway and heave dangerously, with a low, muffled roar, above which is heard JOB ARTHUR'S voice. As he ceases, the roar breaks into a yell, the crowd heaves.

VOICES: Down him, crack the vermin, on top of him, put your foot on the vermin!

ANABEL (with a loud, piercing cry, suddenly starting up): Ah no! Ah no! Ah-h-h-h no-o-o-o! Ah-h-h-h no-o-o-o! Ah-h-h-h no-o-o-o! No-o-o-o! No-o-o-o! No-o! No-o-o! Ah-h-h-h! it's enough, it's enough, it's enough! It's enough, he's a man as you are. He's a man as you are. He's a man as you are. He's a man as you are. (Weeps, a breath of silence.)

OLIVER: Let us stop now, let us stop now. Let me stand up. (Silence.) I want to stand up. (A muffled noise.)

VOICE: Let him get up. (OLIVER rises.)

OLIVER: Be quiet. Be quiet. Now, choose! Choose! Choose! Choose what you will do! Only choose! Choose! it will be irrevocable. (A moment's pause.) Thank God we haven't gone too far. Gerald, get up. (Men still hold him down.)

JOB ARTHUR: Isn't he to answer us? Isn't he going to answer us?

OLIVER: Yes, he shall answer you. He shall answer you. But let him stand up. No more of this. Let him stand up. He must stand up. (Men still hold GERALD down. OLIVER takes hold of their hands and removes them.) Let go, let go now. Yes, let go, yes, I ask you to let go. (Slowly, sullenly, the men let go. GERALD is free, but he does not move.) There, get up, Gerald! Get up! You aren't hurt, are you? You must get up, it's no use. We're doing our best, you must do yours. When things are like this, we have to put up with what we get. (GERALD rises slowly and faces the mob. They roar dully.) You ask why the clerks didn't get this increase? Wait! Wait! Do you still wish for any answer, Mr Freer?

JOB ARTHUR: Yes, that's what we've been waiting for.

OLIVER: Then answer, Gerald.

GERALD: They've trodden on my face.

OLIVER: No matter. Job Arthur will easily answer that you've trodden on their souls. Don't start an altercation. (The crowd is beginning to roar.)

GERALD: You want to know why the clerks didn't get their rise? Because you interfered and attempted to bully about it, do you see. That's why.

VOICES: You want bullying. You'll get bullying, you will.

OLIVER: Can't you see it's no good, either side? It's no mortal use. We might as well all die to-morrow, or to-day, or this minute, as go on bullying one another, one side bullying the other side, and the other side bullying back. We'd better all die.

WILLIE: And a great deal better. I'm damned if I'll take sides with anybody against anything, after this. If I'm to die, I'll die by myself. As for living, it seems impossible.

JOB ARTHUR: Have the men nothing to be said for their side?

OLIVER: They have a great deal, but not everything, you see.

JOB ARTHUR: Haven't they been wronged? And aren't they wronged?

OLIVER: They have, and they are. But haven't they been wrong themselves, too? and aren't they wrong now?

JOB ARTHUR: How?

OLIVER: What about this affair? Do you call it right?

JOB ARTHUR: Haven't we been driven to it?

OLIVER: Partly. And haven't you driven the masters to it, as well?

JOB ARTHUR: I don't see that.

OLIVER: Can't you see that it takes two to make a quarrel? And as long as each party hangs on to its own end of the stick, and struggles to get full hold of the stick, the quarrel will continue. It will continue till you've killed one another. And even then, what better shall you be? What better would you be, really, if you'd killed Gerald Barlow just now? You wouldn't, you know. We're all human beings, after all. And why can't we try really to leave off struggling against one another, and set up a new state of things?

JOB ARTHUR: That's all very well, you see, while you've got the goods.

OLIVER: I've got very little, I assure you.

JOB ARTHUR: Well, if you haven't, those you mix with have. They've got the money, and the power, and they intend to keep it.

OLIVER: As for power, somebody must have it, you know. It only rests with you to put it into the hands of the best men, the men you really believe in. And as for money, it's life, it's living that matters, not simply having money.

JOB ARTHUR: You can't live without money.

OLIVER: I know that. And therefore why can't we have the decency to agree simply about money, just agree to dispose of it so that all men could live their own lives.

JOB ARTHUR: That's what we want to do. But the others, such as Gerald Barlow, they keep the money, and the power.

OLIVER: You see, if you wanted to arrange things so that money flowed more naturally, so that it flowed naturally to every man, according to his needs, I think we could all soon agree. But you don't. What you want is to take it away from one set and give it to another, or keep it yourselves.

JOB ARTHUR: We want every man to have his proper share.

OLIVER: I'm sure I do. I want every man to be able to live and be free. But we shall never manage it by fighting over the money. If you want what is natural and good, I'm sure the owners would soon agree with you.

JOB ARTHUR: What? Gerald Barlow agree with us?

OLIVER: Why not? I believe so.

JOB ARTHUR: You ask him.

OLIVER: Do you think, Gerald, that if the men really wanted a whole, better way, you would agree with them?

GERALD: I want a better way myself, but not their way.

JOB ARTHUR: There, you see!

VOICES: Ah-h! look you! That's him, that's him all over.

OLIVER: You want a better way, but not his way: he wants a better way, but not your way. Why can't you both drop your buts, and simply say you want a better way, and believe yourselves and one another when you say it? Why can't you?

GERALD: Look here! I'm quite as tired of my way of life as you are of yours. If you make me believe you want something better, then I assure you I do: I want what you want. But Job Arthur Freer's not the man to lead you to anything better. You can tell what people want by the leaders they choose, do you see? You choose leaders whom I respect, and I'll respect you, do you see? As it is, I don't. And now I'm going.

VOICES: Who says? Oh ay! Who says goin'?

GERALD: Yes, I'm going. About this affair here we'll cry quits; no more said about it. About a new way of life, a better way all round, I tell you I want it and need it as much as ever you do. I don't care about money really. But I'm never going to be bullied.

VOICE: Who doesn't care about money?

GERALD: I don't. I think we ought to be able to alter the whole system, but not by bullying, not because one lot wants what the other has got.

VOICE: No, because you've got everything.

GERALD: Where's my coat? Now then, step out of the way.

They move towards the car.

CURTAIN

D. H. Lawrence - A Short Biography

David Herbert Lawrence (1885-1930) is today considered to be one of the greatest novelists of the twentieth century writing in the English tongue. He is mostly remembered for his explicit examination of sensual love and sexuality. The latter orientation has subjected his oeuvre to harsh criticism from the conservative literary figures of his time and even to censorship from official authorities. Debates on the literary value of Lawrence's work have outlived him when in the case of the rather "too sensual" *Lady Chatterley's Lover* for instance, an English court had to permit of the publication of the book. However, despite censorship and the moralistic assessments of his works, D. H. Lawrence's merits have been eventually recognized by literary circles. Even critics who frown upon what they consider as the pornographic aspect of some of his writings still rank him among the most serious canonical writers and acknowledge the qualitative contribution that he has brought to the modern novel. It is also noteworthy that besides being a major novelist of the twentieth century, D. H. Lawrence was equally a talented poet, short story writer, literary critic and painter.

D. H. Lawrence was born in 1885 to a poor family living in a coal-mining town near Nottinghamshire, England. He was the youngest of four children with an alcoholic and rather irresponsible father and a mother who venerated knowledge and learning. Being a teacher herself, she wanted Lawrence to get a decent education and did her best to encourage him despite the dire financial conditions in which the family had always found itself. Although he was rather physically weak and sick, Lawrence took after his mother her passion for learning. In 1898, he was the first pupil in town to win a scholarship to Nottingham High School after spending 7 years at the Beauvale Board primary school, now known as D. H. Lawrence Primary School. He soon left high school to serve first as an apprentice clerk at a surgical appliance factory, then as a pupil-teacher. By that time, Lawrence's physical health was deteriorating as he suffered from pneumonia. Only two years after graduating from Nottingham University as a certified teacher in 1908, he lost his mother to whom he was closely related. Some accounts claim that Lawrence practiced euthanasia on his mother to end her suffering from cancer.

During these early years, Lawrence had some attempts at writing poetry and some short stories and to receive early recognition as a young talent, mainly by the *Nottingham Journal*. He also began writing his first novel to be published in 1911 under the title *The White Peacock*. Starting from 1908, Lawrence taught at the Davidson Road School in London while he continued writing poetry and fiction and dreaming of becoming a full-time writer. In London, he was introduced to established writers and publishers who started to appreciate his work and helped him publish his earliest writings. Among these people was the editor of the celebrated periodical *The English Review*. Lawrence was equally encouraged and supervised by the critic and editor Edward Garnett.

After the publication of *The White Peacock* followed by the publication of *The Trespasser* in 1912, Lawrence was working on one of his major works, *Sons and Lovers*. The latter is judged as an autobiographical novel and draws on the author's relationship with his mother. It also pictures the everyday life of working-class England. Lawrence finally resigned from his teaching position by the end of 1911 to devote all his time and energy to his writing career. After being greatly impacted by the loss of his mother and the abandoning of his teaching job, a third crucial event that would shape Lawrence's life and career happened in 1912. It was when he met and fell in love with Frieda Weekley, a German woman who was married and six years older than him. Lawrence and Mrs. Weekley fled England to live in the French-German frontier town of Metz. The couple was able to marry two years later when Frieda got her divorce. The couple spent a period of time in Germany and then moved to Italy to return to Britain on different occasions after their marriage. Later, they wandered different parts of the world, visiting different regions of Italy, Sardinia, Malta, Sri Lanka, Australia and New Wales, to ultimately sail to the United States in 1922.

This long trip around the world was probably triggered at first by the fact that Lawrence suffered from political persecution on more than one occasion in an age dominated by the general hostilities of the First World War. Indeed, in Metz, he was accused of spying for the British and was arrested to be released only after the intercession of Frieda's father. Even at home, Lawrence was suspected mainly for his non-conformist political positions, anti-militarism and unorthodox literary productions, but also for being married to a German lady at a time Nazi Germany was demonized everywhere in Britain.

Sons and Lovers was published in 1913 to realize considerable success. It was followed by the publication of *The Rainbow* in 1915. An important collection of love poems dedicated to Lawrence's love for Frieda was published in 1917 under the title *Look! We Have Come Through*. Critics see in Lawrence's poems a revival of the Romantic tradition tuned in to the modern spirit. In 1916, Lawrence started working on one of his major successes entitled *Women in Love*. Published in 1920, the novel was meant to be a sequel to *The Rainbow*, featuring recurrent characters. It paints the British society of the period while drawing on some details from Lawrence's own life. Some critics believe that the theme of homosexuality in the novel is related to Lawrence's romantic relationship with a farmer from Cornwall. Lawrence's novels were accused of obscenity and found difficulty to be published and distributed. Nevertheless, his merit was recognized by fellow writers such as Ezra Pound and E. M. Forster.

The year 1920 also witnessed the publication of *The Lost Girl* followed by *Aaron's Rod* in 1922 and in which Lawrence provided descriptions of the different places that he had visited as an expatriate. His trip to Australia was, however, best illustrated in his 1923 novel entitled *Kangaroo* which also spoke about the troubles he had with British authorities. Most of the novels of this period bore the influence of the philosopher Friedrich Nietzsche and his theory of the "Superman." Generally, Lawrence was considered to be an elitist who did not believe in the democracy of the masses. His ideals made him the enemy of not only political authorities, but also of many a fellow literary man.

Once in America, the Lawrences were determined to remain there were it not for the author's deteriorating health condition which forced him later to return to the old continent. They acquired a property in New Mexico which is now known as the D. H. Lawrence Ranch. In America, Lawrence befriended Aldous Huxley, another important English writer who would in turn settle in Los Angeles and soon a number of other publications followed. These included *The Boy in the Bush* (1924) and *The Plumed Serpent* (1926). Lawrence became also interested in literary criticism and published a seminal work on American literature entitled *Studies in Classic American Literature*. The volume was believed to revive interest in classic American writers and American literary movements. For later critics, it was a pioneering work written by a British canonical writer on the new literary symbolism of New England, American Puritanism and American Transcendentalism. Another important critical work published by Lawrence was *Study of Thomas hardy and Other Essays*.

By 1925, Lawrence's health no longer allowed him to travel. He had to stay definitively in Florence, Italy, where he published his last books, namely *The Escaped Cock*, *The Virgin and the Gipsy* and the ever-controversial *Lady Chatterley's Lover*. After the agitation caused by the release of the latter novel and accusations of obscenity and cheap pornography, Lawrence vehemently engaged in an extraordinary campaign to defend his writings and to attack those who purport to be the defenders of morals and good taste. This is expressed in many of Lawrence's later prose works and poems. Interestingly, the act of writing with Lawrence was like an act of resistance that continued during his last days and despite his sickness and sufferings. In 1930, D. H. Lawrence was still suffering from pneumonia and tuberculosis. He passed away on March 2nd at the Villa Robermond in Vence, France.

The critical evaluation of Lawrence's oeuvre after his death wavered between praise and hostility before he was definitively established as a canonical English novelist and writer. Critics insisted only on the sexual explicitness of his works and their obsession of obnoxious language and images. However, this tendency left the floor for a more positive artistic assessment, mainly after the historical Lady Chatterley Trial after which Lawrence was proved "not guilty." The trial was a triumph for the idea of sexuality as an object of serious literary exploration and investigation. Indeed, Lawrence's work deals with sex within a social paradigm where politics, economics and aesthetics intervene. Lawrence also deals with the effects of industrialization on human behavior and the shaping of human relationships with emphasis on the role of the body as opposed to the Western overemphasis on the intellect.

Among Lawrence's attempts at non-fiction, there was a book on Freudian psychoanalysis entitled *Psychoanalysis and the Unconscious* (1922) as well as a text book for students published pseudonymously and entitled *Movements in European History*. Once Lawrence's fiction was established as a considerable contribution to canonical English literature, his other merits started to be posthumously acknowledged. These mainly included his talent for poetry as well as his respectable experience as a passionate painter. As for poetry, Lawrence left a huge bulk of material that some estimate to be around 800 poems. In fact, he had been writing poetry since his early childhood until his last years in Florence and France. Among his most famous poems, one can mention "Snake" and "How Beasty the Bourgeoisie is" while celebrated collections include *Dreams Old, Dreams Nascent, Pansies, More Pansies* and *Last Poems*. Like his fiction, Lawrence's verse deal with themes related to industrialization and the eternal struggle between body and mind while still focusing on and exploring sensuality.

D. H. Lawrence had also developed a constant passion for oil painting and was believed to excel in the matter mainly towards his last years. His expressionistic paintings deal with the same themes and motifs as his fiction and poetry. In 1929, a remarkable incident happened when the police confiscated thirteen of his exhibited paintings in a gallery in London. Indeed, the oeuvre was subjected to controversy among artistic circles as well as among politicians and viewpoints ranged between appreciation and praise and accusations of indecency and cheapness. The collection was later regained by its owner on the condition of not exhibiting it in England any more. After Lawrence's death, the collection found its way to Taos in New Mexico to adorn the walls of La Fonda de Taos hotel.

D. H. Lawrence had lived a controversial life and produced highly controversial literary and artistic works to be contested by generations of readers and critics. His confrontational style and his examination of taboo subjects aimed at unveiling the ugly face of false modernity and the ferocity of industrialism that victimized the human in the beginning of the twentieth century. Today, Lawrence represents one of the pillars of twentieth-century literature. The house in Eastwood where he was born and raised in poverty is now the D. H. Lawrence Birthplace and bears testimony to the merits and achievements of a man raised from oblivion to immortality and international recognition.

D.H. Lawrence – A Concise Bibliography

Lawrence's works cover a number of major forms and we have therefore grouped them under convenient headings

Novels

The White Peacock (1911)

The Trespasser (1912)

Sons and Lovers (1913)

The Rainbow (1915)

Women in Love (1920)

The Lost Girl (1920)

Aaron's Rod (1922)

Kangaroo (1923)

The Boy in the Bush (1924)

The Plumed Serpent (1926)

Lady Chatterley's Lover (1928)

The Escaped Cock (1929), later re-published as The Man Who Died

The Virgin and the Gypsy (1930)

Short Story Collections

The Prussian Officer and Other Stories (1914)

England, My England and Other Stories (1922)

The Horse Dealer's Daughter (1922)

The Fox, The Captain's Doll, The Ladybird (1923)

St Mawr and other stories (1925)

The Woman who Rode Away and other stories (1928)

The Rocking-Horse Winner (1926)

The Virgin and the Gipsy and Other Stories (1930)

Love Among the Haystacks and other stories (1930)

Collected Stories (1994) – Everyman's Library

Plays

The Daughter-in-Law (1912)

The Widowing of Mrs Holroyd (1914)

Touch and Go (1920)

David (1926)

The Fight for Barbara (1933)

A Collier's Friday Night (1934)

The Married Man (1940)

The Merry-Go-Round (1941)

Poetry Collections

Love Poems and others (1913)

Amores (1916)

Look! We have come through! (1917)

New Poems (1918)

Bay: a book of poems (1919)

Tortoises (1921)

Birds, Beasts and Flowers (1923)

The Collected Poems of D H Lawrence (1928)

Pansies (1929)

Nettles (1930)

Last Poems (1932)

Fire and other poems (1940)

Non-Fiction Books and Pamphlets

Study of Thomas Hardy and other essays (1914),

Movements in European History (1921)

Psychoanalysis and the Unconscious and Fantasia of the Unconscious (1921/1922)

Studies in Classic American Literature (1923)

Reflections on the Death of a Porcupine and other essays (1925)

A Propos of Lady Chatterley's Lover (1929)

Apocalypse and the writings on Revelation (1931)

Travel Books

Twilight in Italy and Other Essays (1916)

Sea and Sardinia (1921)

Mornings in Mexico and Other Essays (1927)

Sketches of Etruscan Places and other Italian essays (1932)

Works translated by D.H. Lawrence

Lev Isaakovich Shestov All Things are Possible (1920)

Ivan Alekseyevich Bunin The Gentleman from San Francisco (1922)

Giovanni Verga Mastro-Don Gesualdo (1923)

Giovanni Verga Little Novels of Sicily (1925)

Giovanni Verga Cavalleria Rusticana and other stories (1928)

Antonio Francesco Grazzini The Story of Doctor Manente (1929)